Say It Right in
RUSSIAN

Easily Pronounced
Lang~~ Systems, Inc.~~

D1415168

New York   Chicago   San Francisco   Lisbon   London   Madrid   Mexico City
Milan   New Delhi   San Juan   Seoul   Singapore   Sydney   Toronto

Library of Congress Cataloging-in-Publication Data

Say it right in Russian : the easy way to correct pronunciation! / Easily Pronounced
   Language Systems.
         p.   cm. — (Say it right)
      Includes bibliographical references and index.
      ISBN 0-07-149231-3 (alk. paper)
      1. Russian language—Pronunciation by foreign speakers.   2. Russian
language—Spoken Russian.   3. Russian language—Conversation and phrase
books—English.   I. Easily Pronounced Language Systems.
PG2137.S235 2008
491.783′421—dc22   2007032035

5   DIG /DIG 10

ISBN 978-0-07-149231-7
MHID   0-07-149231-3

McGraw-Hill books are available at special quantity discounts to use as
premiums and sales promotions or for use in corporate training programs.
To contact a representative, please visit the Contact Us pages at
www.mhprofessional.com.

Also available: *Say It Right in Arabic • Say It Right in Brazilian Portuguese • Say It
Right in Chinese • Say It Right in French • Say It Right in German • Say It Right in
Italian • Say It Right in Japanese • Say It Right in Korean • Say It Right in Spanish •
Dígalo correctamente en inglés [Say It Right in English]*

Author: Clyde Peters
Illustrations: Luc Nisset
President, EPLS Corporation: Betty Chapman, www.isayitright.com
Senior Series Editor: Priscilla Leal Bailey
Russian Language Consultant: Marya Nikolaevna Kostyleva

This book is printed on acid-free paper.

CONTENTS

INTRODUCTION

The SAY IT RIGHT FOREIGN LANGUAGE PHRASE BOOK SERIES has been developed with the conviction that learning to speak a foreign language should be fun and easy!

All SAY IT RIGHT phrase books feature the EPLS Vowel Symbol System, a revolutionary phonetic system that stresses consistency, clarity, and above all, simplicity!

Since this unique phonetic system is used in all SAY IT RIGHT phrase books, you only have to learn the VOWEL SYMBOL SYSTEM ONCE!

The SAY IT RIGHT series uses the easiest phrases possible for English speakers to pronounce and is designed to reflect how foreign languages are used by native speakers.

You will be amazed at how confidence in your pronunciation leads to an eagerness to talk to other people in their own language.

Whether you want to learn a new language for travel, education, business, study, or personal enrichment, SAY IT RIGHT phrase books offer a simple and effective method of pronunciation and communication.

PRONUNCIATION GUIDE

Most English speakers are familiar with the Russian word **vodka.** This is how the correct pronunciation is represented in the EPLS Vowel Symbol System.

All Russian vowel sounds are assigned a specific non-changing symbol. When these symbols are used in conjunction with consonants and read normally, pronunciation of even the most difficult foreign word becomes incredibly EASY!

On the following page are all the EPLS vowel Symbols used in this book. They are EASY to LEARN since their sounds are familiar. Beneath each symbol are three English words which contain the sound of the symbol.

Practice pronouncing the words under each symbol until you mentally associate the correct vowel sound with the correct symbol. Most symbols are pronounced the way they look!

THE SAME BASIC SYMBOLS ARE USED IN ALL SAY IT RIGHT PHRASE BOOKS!

EPLS VOWEL SYMBOL SYSTEM

(A)
Ace
Bake
Safe

(EE)
See
Fee**t**
Mee**t**

(I)
Ice
Kite
Pie

(O)
Oak
Cold
Sold

(oo)
Cool
Pool
Too

(ah)
Want
Saw
Saw

(ĕ)
Men
Red
Bed

(i)
Win
Sit
Give

(ow)
Cow
How
Now

(oy)
Boy
Toy
Joy

(EE)

This EPLS vowel symbol has been narrowed to indicate visually that this sound is barely pronounced. On the next page we will explain its importance.

EPLS VOWEL SYMBOL ENHANCEMENTS

On the previous page are all the EPLS Vowel Symbols used in this book. They are EASY to LEARN since their sounds are familiar.

On page x you will find the Cyrillic alphabet listed along with the EPLS Vowel Symbol or Consonant that represents the Cyrillic letter or letters.

EPLS has enhanced the following symbol below to visually help you recognize that this sound is shortened.

When a narrow symbol appears before any other symbol (example below) it reminds you to barely pronounce this vowel sound like the **ie** in fi**e**sta.

EXAMPLE: The Russian word for "no" is:

N⒠ěT

EPLS CONSONANTS

Consonants are letters like **T**, **D**, and **K**. They are easy to recognize and their pronunciation seldom changes. The following pronunciation guide letters represent some Cyrillic consonants and their EPLS equivalents.

R   Pronounce this **EPLS** letter like the rolled Spanish **r**.

ZH   Pronounce these **EPLS** letters like **s** in mea**s**ure.

LD   Pronounce this **EPLS** letter like the **ld** in co**ld**.

ZD   Pronounce these **EPLS** letters like the letters **sed** in plea**sed**.

H   Pronounce this **EPLS** letter like the **h** in **ha** preceded by a puff of air making an aspirated **H** sound.

Y   Pronounce this **EPLS** letter like the **ye** in **ye**s or the **ya** in **ya**cht.

MN   Pronounce these **EPLS** letters like the **mn** in o**mn**i.

SHCH   You have to run these four consonants together. No way around it! Try to isolate the letters in the words fi**shch**ips.

THE CYRILLIC ALPHABET

The Cyrillic alphabet has 33 letters. Below is the entire alphabet, which is easily represented by an EPLS letter or symbol. As you read through the book you will start to assimilate this alphabet. Although the Cyrillic letters are fairly consistent, pronunciation will change depending on position and various grammatical rules.

Аа	ah	as in s**aw**
Бб	B	as in **b**ed
Вв	V	as in **v**an
Гг	G	as in **g**ood
Дд	D	as in **d**og
Ее	Y€	as in **ye**t
Ёё	YO	as in **Yo**
Жж	ZH	as in plea**s**ure
Зз	Z	as in **z**oo
Ии	EE	as in **e**at
Йй	oy	as in b**oy**
Кк	K	as in **k**eep
Лл	L	as in **l**ake
Мм	M	as in **m**om
Нн	N	as in **n**oon
Оо	O	as in **o**ak
	ah	as in **o**ff
Пп	P	as in **p**eg
Рр	R	as in **r**un
Сс	S	as in **s**ee
Тт	T	as in **t**ie

Уу	oo	as in **oo**ps
Фф	F	as in **f**un
Хх	H as in **h**ot, but guttural
Цц	TS	as in hi**ts**
Чч	CH	as in **ch**air
Шш	SH	as in **sh**oe
Щщ	SHCH	as in fi**shch**ips
Ъъ	hard sign: has no sound of its own but affects other sounds.
Ыы	i/EE as in **i**f or **e**at
Ьь	soft sign: has no sound of its own but affects other sounds.
Ээ	€ as in **e**nd
Юю	Yoo as in **you**
Яя	Yah as in **ya**wn

PRONUNCIATION TIPS

- Each pronunciation guide word is broken into syllables. Read each word slowly, one syllable at a time, increasing speed as you become more familiar with the system.

- In Russian it is extremely important to emphasize certain syllables. This mark (´) over the syllable reminds you to STRESS that syllable.

- If you do not pay attention to the stressed symbol you can easily change the meaning of the word.

- In Russian the syllables following the stressed symbol tend to be spoken lightly in a faded-out manner.

- In the spoken language, the pronunciation of a particular letter will be affected by the letters in front of it or directly following.

- Take a little time to familiarize yourself with the Cyrillic letters on the previous page. Note that there are no articles such as **a**, **an**, and **the** in Russian.

- To perfect your Russian accent you must listen closely to Russian speakers and adjust your speech accordingly.

- The pronunciation choices in this book were chosen for their simplicity and effectiveness.

ICONS USED IN
THIS BOOK

 ## KEY WORDS

You will find this icon at the beginning of chapters indicating key words
relating to chapter content. These are
important words to become familiar
with.

 ## PHRASEMAKER

The Phrasemaker icon provides the
traveler with a choice of phrases that
allows the user to make his or her
own sentences.

Say It Right in
RUSSIAN

ESSENTIAL WORDS AND PHRASES

Here are some basic words and phrases that will help you express your needs and feelings in **Russian**.

Hi

Привет

PR(EE)-V(EE)(ё)'T

Hello

Здравствуйте (polite)

ZDR(ah)-STV(oo)-Y(ё)-T(EE)(EE)

How are you?

Как вы поживаете?

K(ah)K V(EE) P(ah)-ZH(EE)-V(ah)'-Y(ё)-T(EE)(EE)

Fine, thank you.

Хорошо, спасибо.

H(ah)-R(ah)-SH(O)' SP(ah)-S(EE)'-B(ah)

And you?	**Good-bye**
А вы?	До свидания
(ah) V(EE)	D(ah)-SV(EE)-D(ah)'-NY(ah)

Good morning

Доброе утро

DO͞-BRah-Yē͞ o͞o-TRah

Good afternoon

Добрый день

DO͞-BRēē Dēē͞N

Good evening

Добрый вечер

DO͞-BRēē Vēē͞-CHēR

Good night

Спокойной ночи

SPah-Koy-NI͞ NO͞-CHēē

Mr. (literally: young man)

Молодой человек

Mah-Lah-Doy CHē-Lah-Vēē͞K

Mrs. / Miss (literally: young woman)

Девушка

Dē͞-Voo SH-Kah

Ma'am (older woman)

Бабушка

Bah-Boo SH-Kah

Yes

Да

D@h

No

Нет

N@@T

Please

Пожалуйста

P@h-ZH@h-L@-ST@h

Thank you

Спасибо

SP@h-S@-B@h

Excuse me

Извините

@Z-V@-N@-T@@

I'm sorry

Простите

PR@h-ST@-T@@

I don't understand!

Я не понимаю!

Y@h N㏄-P@h-N㏄-M@h-Y㏄

Do you understand?

Вы меня понимаете?

V㏄ M㏄-NY@h
P@h-N㏄-M@h-Y㏔-T㏄㏔

I'm a tourist.

Я турист.

Y@h T㏄-R㏄ST

I don't understand Russian.

Я не понимаю по-русски.

Y@h N㏄-P@h-N㏄-M@h-Y㏄
P@h-R㏄S-K㏄

Do you speak English?

Вы по-английски говорите?

V㏄ P@h-@hN-GL㏄-SK㏄
G@h-V@h-R㏄-T㏄㏔

Please repeat.

Повторите, пожалуиста.

P@hF-T@h-R㏄-T㏄㏔
P@h-ZH@h-L㏄-ST@h

FEELINGS

I would like...(male speaking)

Я бы хотел...

Yah BWEE Hah-TEEёL...

I would like...(female speaking)

Я бы хотела...

Yah BWEE Hah-TEEё-Lah...

I want...

Я хочу...

Yah Hah-CHoo...

I have...

У меня есть...

oo-MEE-NYah YёST...

I know.	**I don't know.**
Я знаю.	Я не знаю.
Yah ZNah-Yoo	Yah NEE-ZNah-Yoo

I like it.

Мне это нравится.

MNEё ё-Tah NRah-VEE-TSah

I don't like it.

Мне это не нравится.

MNEё ё-Tah NEE-NRah-VEE-TSah

I'm lost. (male speaking)

Я потерялся.

Yah Pah-Tē-Rēah'L-Sēah

I'm lost. (female speaking)

Я потерялась.

Yah Pah-Tē-Rēah'-Lah S

We are lost.

Мы потерялись.

MWēē Pah-Tē-Rēah'-Lēē S

I'm ill. (male speaking)

Я болен.

Yah BŌ'-Lēn

I'm ill. (female speaking)

Я больна.

Yah Bah L-Nah'

I'm hungry. (male speaking)

Я голоден.

Yah GŌ'-Lah-Dēn

I'm hungry. (female speaking)

Я голодна.

Yah Gah-Lah D-Nah'

INTRODUCTIONS

Use the following phrases when meeting someone for the first time both privately and in business.

My name is...

Меня зовут...

MEE-NYah Zah-VOoT...

What's your name?

Как вас зовут?

KahK VahS Zah-VOoT

Very nice to meet you.

Было приятно познакомиться.

BWEE-Lah PREE-YahT-Nah
PahZ-Nah-KO-MEE-TSah

GENERAL GUIDELINES

Russia is the largest country on the planet and tourism has taken off since the dissolution of the Soviet Union. It is a nation spanning eleven time zones and two continents.

- In Russia, don't expect a lot of smiles when you meet, however, Russians like to stand closer than Americans are accustomed to.

- Giving a Russian the "OK" sign is considered rude.

- Hand shaking is common practice, both on arrival and taking leave.

- Public bear hugs are normal.

- Friendship with a Russian is not to be treated lightly.

- Hospitality is a great Russian virtue. An invitation to a Russian's home is a real treat and education into the true meaning of hospitality.

- Toasts are usually given at the beginning of the meal and very long meals are quite common.

THE BIG QUESTIONS

Who?
Кто?

KT◎

Who is it?
Кто это?

KT◎ ё́-T@h

What?
Что?

SHT◎

What's that?
Что это?

SHT◎ ё́-T@h

When?
Когда?

K@hG-D@h́

Where?
Где?

GDYё̆

Where is...?

Где...?

GDYⒺ...

Which?

Какой?   Который?

KⒶ-KⓄⓎ   KⒶ-TⓄ-RⒺⒺ

Why?

Почему?

PⒶ-CHⒺⒺ-MⓄⓄ

How?

Как?

KⒶK

How much? (money)

Сколько?

SKⓄL-KⒶ

How long? (time)

Как долго?

KⒶK DⓄL-GⒶ

ASKING FOR THINGS

The following phrases are valuable for directions, food, help, etc. When asking a question, it is polite to say "Could I ask?" and "Thank you."

I would like...(male speaking)

Я бы хотел...

Y@h BW@ H@h-T@@'L...

I would like...(female speaking)

Я бы хотела...

Y@h BW@ H@h-T@@'-L@h...

I need...

Мне нужно...

MN@@ N@@'ZH-N@h...

Can you...?

Не могли бы вы...?

N@@-M@hG-L@@' BW@ V@@...

Could I ask?	Thank you.
Можно вас спросить?	Спасибо.
M@'ZH-N@h	SP@h-S@@-B@h
V@hS SPR@h-S@@'T	

PHRASEMAKER

I would like...(male speaking)

Я хотел бы...

Y@h H@h-T㐀L BW㒀...

I would like...(female speaking)

Я хотела бы...

Y@h H@h-T㐀-L@h BW㒀...

▶ **more coffee**

ещё кофе

Y㒀-SH㋒́ K㋒́-F㐀

▶ **some water**

воды

V@h-D㒀́

▶ **some ice**

льда

LD@h

▶ **the menu**

меню

M㐀-N㋓́

PHRASEMAKER

Here are a few sentences
you can use when you feel
the urge to say **I need**... or **can you**...?

I need...

Мне нужно...

MN⒠⒠ N⓪⓪ZH-N⒜...

> ▷ **more money**

больше денег

B⓪L-SH⒠ D⒠-N⒠K

> ▶ **change** (money)

разменять

R⒜Z-M⒠-N⒠⒠T

I need your help.

Мне нужна ваша помощь.

MN⒠⒠ N⓪ZH-N⒜ V⒜-SH⒜ P⓪-M⒜SH

I need a doctor.

Мне нужен врач.

MN⒠⒠ N⓪⓪-ZH⒠N VR⒜CH

I need a lawyer.

Мне нужен адвокат

MN⒠⒠ N⓪⓪-ZH⒠N ⒜D-V⒜-K⒜T

PHRASEMAKER

Can you...

Вы можете...

VEE MO'-ZHĕ-Tĕĕ...

▶ **help me?**

помочь мне?

Pah-MO'CH MNĕĕĕ

▶ **give me...?**

дать мне...?

DahT MNĕĕĕ...

▶ **tell me...?**

сказать мне...?

SKah-Zah'T MNĕĕĕ...

▶ **take me to...?**

отвезти меня...?

ahT-VEE-STEE MEE-NYah'...

ASKING THE WAY

No matter how independent
you are, sooner or later you'll
probably have to ask for directions.

Where is...?

Где...?

GDYⓔ...

I'm looking for...

Я ищу...

Yⓐ   ⒺⒺ-SHⓞⓞ...

Is it near?

Это близко?

ⓔ-Tⓐ   BLⒺⒺZ-Kⓐ

Is it far?

Это далеко?

ⓔ-Tⓐ   Dⓐ-Lⓔ-Kⓞ

Left	**Right**
Левый	Правый
Lⓔ-VⒺⒺ	PRⓐ-VⒺⒺ

PHRASEMAKER

Where is...

Где...

GDY@...

▶ **the restroom?**

туалет?

T@@-L@T

▶ **the telephone?**

телефон?

T@-L@-F@N

▶ **the beach?**

пляж?

PL@@ZH

▶ **the hotel?**

гостиница?

G@S-T@-N@-TS@

▶ **the train for...?**

поезд на...?

P@-Y@ST N@...

Note: In Russian there are no articles like **a**, **an** or **the** as used in the English sentences above.

TIME

What time is it?

Который сейчас час?

Kah-TO-REE SEE-CHahS CHahS

Morning

Утро

oo-TRah

Noon

Полдень

POL-DeN

Night

Ночь

NOCH

Today

Сегодня

SEE-VOD-NYah

Tomorrow

Завтра

ZahF-TRah

This week

На этой неделе

Nah ẽ-Tẽİ NEE-Dẽ-Lẽ

This month

В этом месяце

Vẽ-TahM Mẽ-SEE-TSẽ

This year

В этом году

Vẽ-TahM Gah-Doo

Now

Сейчас

SEE-CHahS

Soon

Скоро

SKO-Rah

Later

Позже

PO-ZHẽ

Never

Никогда

NEE-KahG-Dah

WHO IS IT?

I

Я

Y(ah)

You (polite)	**You** (informal)
Вы	Ты
V(ee)	T(ee)

He / She / It

Он / Она / Оно

(O)N / (ah)-N(ah) / (ah)-N(O)

We

Мы

MW(ee)

You (plural)

Вы

V(ee)

They

Они

(ah)-N(ee)

THIS AND THAT

The equivalents of **this, that, these,** and **which** are as follows:

This

Это

Ė-Tah

This is mine.

Это моё.

Ė-Tah Mah-YÓ

That

Тот

TOT

That is mine.

То моё.

TO Mah-YÓ

These

Эти

Ė-TEE

These are mine.

Эти мои.

Ė-TEE Mah-EÉ

USEFUL OPPOSITES

Near	**Far**
Близко	Далеко
BL㈎S-K㋐	D㋐-L㧐-K㋡

Here	**There**
Здесь	Там
ZD㧐S	T㋐M

Left	**Right**
Левый	Правый
L㧐-V㈎	PR㋐-V㈎

A little	**A lot**
Немного	Много
N㧐M-N㋡-G㋐	MN㋡-G㋐

More	**Less**
Больше	Меньше
B㋡L-SH㈎㧐	M㧐N-SH㈎

Big	**Small**
Большой	Маленький
B㋐L-SH㋒	M㋐-L㈎N-K㈎

Open	**Closed**
Открыто	Закрыто
ⓐⓗT-KRⒺⒺ́-Tⓐⓗ	Zⓐⓗ-KRⒺⒺ́-Tⓐⓗ

Cheap	**Expensive**
Дешевый	Дорогой
DⒺⒺ-SHⓄ́-VⒺⒺ	Dⓐⓗ-Rⓐⓗ-GⓄⓨ́

Dirty	**Clean**
Грязный	Чистый
GRYⓐⓗ́Z-NⒺⒺ	CHⒺⒺ́-STⒺⒺ

Good	**Bad**
Хороший	Плохой
Hⓐⓗ-RⓄ́-SHⒺⒺ	PLⓐⓗ-HⓄⓨ́

Vacant	**Occupied**
Вакантный	Занятый
Vⓐⓗ-Kⓐⓗ́NT-NⒺⒺ	Zⓐⓗ́-NⒺⒺ̇ⓐⓗ-TⒺⒺ

Right	**Wrong**
Правильно	Неправильно
PRⓐⓗ́-VⒺⒺL-Nⓐⓗ	NⒺⒺ-PRⓐⓗ́-VⒺⒺL-Nⓐⓗ

WORDS OF ENDEARMENT

I like you.

Ты мне нравишься.

TEE MNEE NRah-VEESH-Sah

I love you.

Я тебя люблю.

Yah TEE-Bah Loo-BLoo

I love Russia.

Я люблю Россию.

Yah Loo-BLoo Rah-SEE-Yoo

Male friend

Друг

DRooK

Female friend

Подруга

Pah-DRoo-Gah

Kiss me!

Поцелуй меня!

Pah-TSe-Looee MEE-NYah

WORDS OF ANGER

What do you want?

Что вам нужо?

SHT⓪ VⓐM Nⓞ֯ZH-Nⓐ

Leave me alone!

Оставь меня в покое!

ⓐS-Tⓐ֩F M⒠⒠-NYⓐ֩ FPⓐ-K⓸֩-Yⓐ

Go away!

Уходи!

⓸-Hⓐ-D⒠⒠֩

Be quiet!

Тише!

T⒠⒠֩-SH⒠

That's enough!

Хватит!

HV⒠⒠֩-T⒠⒠T

COMMON EXPRESSIONS

When you are at a loss for words but have the feeling you should say something, try one of these!

No problem.

Хорошо.

H⒜-R⒜-SHO͞

Ok!

Ладно.

L⒜D-N⒜

Never mind!

Забудь!

Z⒜-B○○D

Ouch!

Ай!

Ⓘ

Great job!

Молодец!

M⒜-L⒜-D⒠TS

Good luck!

Удачи!

@-Dah-CHEE

My goodness!

Боже мой!

BO-ZHe Moy

How beautiful!

Как красиво!

KahK KRah-SEE-Vah

Of course!

Конечно!

Kah-NeeeSH-Nah

What a shame!

Как жаль!

KahK ZHahL

Bravo!

Браво!

BRah-Vah

USEFUL COMMANDS

Stop!

Стой!

ST@y

Go! (by vehicle)

Езжай!

Y©-ZH①

Go! (by foot)

Иди!

©-D©

Wait!

Подожди!

P@-D@ZH-D©

Slow down!

Медленее!

M©D-L©-N©-©

Come here!

Подойди!

P@-D①-D©

EMERGENCIES

Fire!

Пожар!

P@h-ZH@hR

Help!

Помогите!

P@h-M@h-GEE-TEE-ĕ

Hurry!

Скорее!

SK@h-RĕY-Yĕ

Call the police!

Вызовите милицию!

VEE-Z@h-VEE-TEE-ĕ   MEE-LEE-TSEE-Yoo

Call an ambulance!

Вызовите скорую помощь!

VEE-Z@h-VEE-TEE-ĕ

SKO-Roo-Yoo   PO-M@hSH

ARRIVAL

Passing through customs should be easy since there are usually agents available who speak English. You may be asked how long you intend to stay and if you have anything to declare.

- Have your passport ready.

- Be sure all documents are up-to-date.

- You will be required to fill out a customs form declaring personal items you are bringing into the country. It is very important to hold on to this form and present it when leaving Russia.

- It is important to note that you will not be allowed to leave Russia with more money than you declared on arrival.

- While in Russia, it is wise to keep receipts for everything you buy as well as ask for a certificate from shop owners showing that you paid for items with hard currency.

- If you have connecting flights, be sure to reconfirm in advance and arrive 2 to 3 hours early for flights and lengthy customs processing.

- Make sure your luggage is clearly marked inside and out and always keep an eye on it when in public places.

KEY WORDS

Baggage

Багаж

B@-G@ZH

Customs

Таможня

T@-M@ZH-NY@

Documents

Документы

D@-K@-M@@N-T@

Passport

Паспорт

P@S-P@RT

Porter

Носильщик

N@-S@L-SH@K

Taxi

Такси

T@K-S@

USEFUL PHRASES

Here is my passport.

Вот мой паспорт.

VOT MOY PAHS-PAHRT

I have nothing to declare.

Мне нечего декларировать.

MNYĕ Nĕ-CHĔĕ-Vah
Dĕ-KLah-RĔ-Rah-VahT

I'm here on business.

Я здесь по бизнесу.

Yah ZDĕS Pah-BĔZ-Nĕ-Soo

I'm on vacation.

Я в отпуске.

Yah VOT-Poos-Kĕĕ

Is there a problem?

Какие-то проблемы?

Kah-KĔ-Yĕ-Tah PRah-BLĔĕ-MỈ
TahM PRah-BLYĕ-Mah

PHRASEMAKER

I'll be staying...

Я здесь буду...

Y@ ZD®S B☺-D☺...

▸ **one night**

ночь

N☉CH

▸ **two nights**

двое суток

DV☉́-Y® S☺-T@K

▸ **one week**

неделю

N®-D®®́-L☺

▸ **two weeks**

две недели

DV®® N®-D®́-L®

USEFUL PHRASES

I need a porter.

Мне нужен носильщик.

MNⒺⒺ NⓄⓄ-ZHⒺ̃N Nⓐ-SⒺⒺL-SHⒾK

These are my bags.

Вот мои сумки.

VⓄT Mⓐ̈Ⓔ-SⓄⓄM-KⒺ

Can you help me with my luggage please?

Будьте добры, помогите мне
с багажом.

BⓄⓄ-TYⒺ̃ Dⓐ-BRⓄ
Pⓐ-Mⓐ-GⒺⒺ-TⒺ̃Ⓔ̃ MNⒺⒺ
ZBⓐ-Gⓐ-ZHⓄM

I'm missing a bag.

У меня потерялась сумка.

ⓄⓄ-MⒺⒺ-NYⓐ
Pⓐ-TⒺⒺ-RⒺ̈ⓐ-Lⓐ̈S SⓄⓄM-Kⓐ

Thank you. This is for you.

Спасибо. Это вам.

SPⓐ-SⒺⒺ-Bⓐ Ⓔ̃-Tⓐ Vⓐ̈M

PHRASEMAKER

Where is...

Где...

GDY℮...

▶ **customs?**

таможня?

T@h-MO͞ZH-NY@h

▶ **baggage claim?**

выдача багажа?

VO͜I-D@h-CH@h B@h-G@h-ZH@h

▶ **a taxi stand?**

такси?

T@hK-SE͞E͞

▶ **the bus stop?**

автобусная остановка?

@hF-TO͞-Bo͞oS-N@h-Y@h

@hS-T@h-NO͞F-K@h

HOTEL SURVIVAL

A wide selection of accommodations is available.in major cities. The most complete range of facilities is found in five star hotels.

- Make reservations well in advance and request the address of the hotel to be written in Russian as most taxi drivers do not speak English.

- Do not leave valuables or cash in your room when you are not there!

- Electrical items like blow-dryers may be provided by your hotel, however, you may want to purchase small electrical appliances there.

- It is a good idea to make sure you give your room number to persons you expect to call you. This can avoid confusion with western names.

- You will receive an immigrant card on your flight to Russia. You must register your Immigrant Card with your hotel on arrival.

KEY WORDS

Hotel

Гостиница

Gah-STEE-NEE-TSah

Bellman

Швейцар

SHVEE-TSahR

Maid

Горничная

GOR-NEECH-Nah-Yah

Message

Сообщение

Sah-ahP-SHCHE-NEE

Reservation

Бронирование

BRah-NEE-Rah-Vah-NEE

Room service

Обслуживание номера

ahB-SLOO-ZHEE-Vah-NEE-YE
NO-ME-Rah

CHECKING IN

My name is...

Меня зовут...

M⒠-NY⒜ Z⒜-V⓪T...

I have a reservation.

У меня забронирован номер.

⓪-M⒠-NY⒜
Z⒜-B⒭⒜-N⒠-⒭⒜-V⒜N N⓪-M⒠⒭

Have you any vacancies?

У вас есть вакантные номера?

⓪-V⒜S Y⒠ST
V⒜-K⒜N-TN⓪-Y⒠ N⒜-M⒠-⒭⒜

What is the charge per night?

Сколько стоит за сутки?

SK⓪L-K⒜ ST⓪-⓪T Z⒜ S⓪T-K⒠

My room key, please.

Мой ключ от номера, пожалуйста.

M⒪ KL⓪CH ⒜T N⓪-M⒠-⒭⒜
P⒜-ZH⒜-L⓪-ST⒜

PHRASEMAKER

I would like a room with...(male speaking)

Я бы хотел номер...

Y@h BW©© H@h-T®©́L NО́-M®B...

I would like a room with...(female speaking)

Я бы хотела номер...

Y@h BW©© H@h-T®©́-L@h NО́-M®B...

▶ **a bath**

с ванной

SV@́N-NО̀

▶ **one bed**

одноместный

@hD-N@h-M®́S-N©©

▶ **two beds**

двуместный

DV©©-M®́S-N©©

▶ **a shower**

с душем

ZD©©́-SH®M

USEFUL PHRASES

I need an extra key.

Мне нужен запасной ключ.

MNⒺⒺ NⓄⓄ-ZHⒺN

Zⓐⱨ-PⓐⱨS-NⓄⓎ KLⓄⓄCH

Are there any messages for me?

Есть ли сообщения для меня?

YⒺST-LⒺⒺ Sⓐⱨ-ⓐⱨP-SHCHⒺ-NⒺⒺ

DLⓐⱨ MⒺⒺ-NYⓐⱨ

Where is the dining room?

Где столовая?

GDYⒺ STⓐⱨ-LⓄ-Vⓐⱨ-Yⓐⱨ

Are meals included?

Входит ли еда в цену?

FHⓄ-DⒺⒺT LⒺⒺ YⒺ-Dⓐⱨ

FTSⒺ-NⓄⓄ

At what time is breakfast?

Во сколько завтрак?

Vⓐⱨ-SKⓄL-Kⓐⱨ ZⓐⱨF-TRⓐⱨK

PHRASEMAKER
(WAKE UP CALL)

Please wake me at...

Разбудите меня, пожалуйста...

R@hZ-B@-D@E-T@@ M@E-NY@h
P@h-ZH@h-L@-ST@h...

▸ **6:00 a.m.**
в шесть часов
FSH@ST CH@h-S@F

▸ **6:30 a.m.**

в половине седьмого

FP@h-L@h-V@E-NY@ S@D-M@-V@h

▸ **7:00 a.m.**
в семь часов
FS@@M CH@h-S@F

▸ **7:30 a.m.**

в половине восьмого

FP@h-L@h-V@E-N@@ V@hS-M@-V@h

▸ **8:00 a.m.**

в восемь часов

V@-S@@M CH@h-S@F

PHRASEMAKER

I need...

Мне нужно...

MNEEE   NooZH-Nah...

▶ **clean sheets**

чистое постельное бельё

CHEES-Tah-YE   PahS-TEEEL-Nah-YE
BEL-YO

▶ **more blankets**

больше одеял

BOL-SHE   ah-DE-YahL

▶ **more towels**

болше полотенец

BOL-SHE   Pah-Lah-TE-NETS

▶ **soap**

мыло

MWEE-Lah

I need a hotel safe.

Мне нужен сейф.

MNYẽ NOO'-ZHẽN SAF

I need the manager.

Мне нужен заведующий.

MNẽẽ NOO-ZHẽN Zah-Vẽ'-Doo-Yoo-SHẽ

I need a bellman.

Мне нужен швейцар.

MNẽẽ NOO-ZHẽN SHVẽ-TSahʹR

I need a maid

Мне нужна горничная

MNẽẽ NOOʹZH-Nah GOʹR-NẽCH-Nah-Yah

I need a babysitter.

Мне нужна няня.

MNẽẽ NOOZH-Nahʹ Nẽahʹ-Nẽah

I need ice cubes.

Мне нужны кубики льда.

MNẽẽ NOO-ZHĩʹ KOO-Bẽ-Kẽ LDah

I need toilet paper.

Мне нужна туалетная бумага.

MNẽẽ NOOZH-Nahʹ

TOO-ah-LẽẽʹT-Nah-Yah BOO-Mahʹ-Gah

PHRASEMAKER
(PROBLEMS)

There is no...

Нет...

N@@@T...

▶ **electricity**

электричества

@-L@K-TR@-CH@ST-V@h

▶ **heat**

отопления

@h-T@P-L@-N@-Y@h

▶ **hot water**

горячей воды

G@h-R@@h-CH@-Y@   V@h-D@

▶ **light**

света

SV@@-T@h

▶ **toilet paper**

туалетной бумаги

T@-@h-L@@T-N①   B@-M@h-G@

PHRASEMAKER
(SPECIAL NEEDS)

Do you have...?

У вас есть...?

ⓞⓞ-Vⓐ̲S Yⓔ̲ST...

▸ **an elevator?**

лифт?

Lⓔ̲FT

▸ **a ramp?**

съезд?

Sⓔ̲ⓔ̲ST

▸ **a wheel chair?**

инвалидное кресло?

ⓔ̲N-Vⓐ̲-Lⓔ̲D-Nⓐ̲-Yⓔ̲ KRⓔ̲S-Lⓐ̲

▸ **facilities for the disabled?**

номера для инвалидов?

Nⓐ̲-Mⓔ̲-Rⓐ̲ DLYⓐ̲

ⓔ̲N-Vⓐ̲-Lⓔ̲-Dⓐ̲F

CHECKING OUT

The bill, please.

Счёт, пожалуйста.

SH⊙T P⒜-ZH⒜'-L⊚⊚-ST⒜

There is a mistake!

Здесь ошибка!

ZD⒠S ⒜-SH⒠⒠P-K⒜

Do you accept credit cards?

Вы принимаете кредитные карточки?

V⒠⒠ PR⒠⒠-N⒠⒠-M⒜-Y⒠-T⒠⒠

KR⒠-D⒠⒠T-N⒠⒠ K⒜R-T⒜CH-K⒠⒠

Could you have my luggage brought down?

Не могли бы вы снести мой багаж вниз?

N⒠-M⒜G-L⒠⒠' BW⒠⒠ V⒠⒠

SN⒠⒠-ST⒠⒠' M⒪⒴

B⒜-G⒜'ZH VN⒠⒠S

Please call a taxi.

Пожалуйста, вызовите такси.

P@h-ZH@h-L@@-ST@h
V©©-Z@h-V©©-T©© T@hK-S©©

I had a very good time! (male speaking)

Я очень хорошо провёл время!

Y@h O-CH©N H@h-R@h-SHO
PR@h-V©©L VR©-MY@h

I had a very good time! (female speaking)

Я очень хорошо провёл время!

Y@h O-CH©N H@h-R@h-SHO
PR@h-V©©-L@h VR©-MY@h

Thanks for everything.

Спасибо за всё.

SP@h-S©©-B@h Z@h-VS©©O

We'll see you next time.

До следующей встречи.

D@h-SL©©©-D@@-SH@ FSTR©-CH©©

Good-bye.

До свидания.

D@h-SV©©-D@h-NY@h

RESTAURANT SURVIVAL

Tasting Russian cuisine is a taste of Russian history. Enjoy Russian specialties such as borsch and akroshka (soup), ponchiki (donuts), blini (pancakes), and pelmeni as well as many other wonderful specialties.

- Russians eat breakfast between 7 AM and 8 AM, and lunch from 1:30 PM to 2:30 PM. Supper is usually served from 7:00 PM to 9:00 PM.

- Pirozhki, meat or vegetable pies, are sold on street corners.

- Breakfast is usually boiled eggs, bread and cold meats. Lunch and dinner menus will vary. Borsch is a traditional beetroot soup served with sour cream. This soup is served hot. A sister soup is akroshka made from cucumbers.

- Eating, drinking and entertainment are at the heart of the Russian dining experience. Bread plays a very important role in Russian cuisine and dinner can run as long as three hours.

- Tipping is not expected but is greatly appreciated.

KEY WORDS

Breakfast

Завтрак

Z@F-TR@K

Lunch

Обед

@-B@@T

Dinner

Ужин

@-ZH@N

Waiter

Официант

@-F@-TS@-@NT

Waitress

Официантка

@-F@-TS@-@NT-K@

Restaurant

Ресторан

R@-ST@-R@N

USEFUL PHRASES

A table for...

Стол для...

ST◎L DLY@...

2	4	6
двоих	четверых	шестерых
DV@EEH	CH@-TV@E-B◯H	SH@-ST@-B◯H

The menu, please.

Меню, пожалуйста.

M@-NY◎ P@-ZH@-L◎-ST@

Separate checks, please.

Нам, пожалуйста, отдельные чеки.

N@M P@-ZH@-L◎-ST@

@-D@L-N@@ CH@-K@

We are in a hurry.

Мы спешим.

MW@ SP@-SH@M

What do you recommend?

Что вы порекомендуете?

SHT◎ V@

P@-B@-K@-M@N-D◎-Y@-T@

Please bring me...

Принесите мне, пожалуйста...

PREE-NEE-SEE'-TEE MNEE
Pah-ZHah'-LOOS-Tah...

Please bring us...

Принесите нам, пожалуйста...

PREE-NEE-SEE'-TEE NahM
Pah-ZHah'-LOO-STah...

I'm hungry. (male speaking)	**I'm hungry.** (female speaking)
Я голоден.	Я голодна.
Yah GO'-Lah-DEN	Yah Gah-Lah-DNah'

I'm thirsty.

Хочется пить.

HO'-CHEE-TSah PEET

Is service included?

Обслуживание входит в счёт?

ahP-SLOO-ZHEE-Vah-NEE
FHO'-DEET FSHOT

The bill, please.

Счёт, пожалуйста.

SHOT Pah-ZHah'-LOO-STah

RUSSIAN CUISINES AND STYLES

Russian food is quite different from American food and more difficult to prepare. Russian cuisine is famous for exotic soups, cabbage schi and solyanka, and can be made with assorted meats. Meat and potatoes are also very popular.

Russians are great lovers of bread with its richness, health properties and wonderful aromas. The favorite bread is rye and Russians consume more of it than any other country in the world.

One specialty is tasty traditional Russian pelmeni. Pelmeni basically consist of a flour envelope mixture filled with tender pork and served in broth. Pelmeni, piroshki and blini are very popular meals in Russia.

Eating, drinking and entertainment personify the soul of Russian mealtime. Russian wheat vodka is the world's best, and the Russian table is not complete without a bottle: from clear, colorless Moskovskaya to many bitters.

Kvas is a well-known and very popular national non-alcoholic drink. This refreshing summer drink can also be found in flavors of apple, raspberry and raisin. It is wise to mention here that kvas is an acquired taste.

EATING ESTABLISHMENTS

Restaurant or Restoran

"Restaurant" is clearly defined in Russia by its excellence and food specialties including quality champagnes, wines, and vodkas and in most cases entertainment.

In Moscow and St. Petersburg you will find more foods of American influence as well as other cuisines such as Chinese, French, Italian etc. It is important to note that portions are very small.

Café or Kafe

"Cafés" are usually small and informal. They can range from small well-appointed restaurants offering steak and lobster to a basic coffee shop serving drinks, pastries and ice cream, but not coffee. Late opening times of cafés offer a relaxing and enjoyable atmosphere for the evening and some provide entertainment.

Grill Bar or Gril Bar

Drinks, grilled meats, often chicken are offered here and some gril bars offer shashlik or shish kebab.

Beer Bar or Pivnoy Bar

Serves beer and appetizers, however, a **beer restaurant** offers a more extensive menu.

BEVERAGE LIST

Coffee

кофе

KO-Fĕ

Decaffeinated coffee

декафеиновый кофе

DEE-Kah-FEE-EE-Nah-VEE   KO-Fĕ

Tea

чай

CHI

Cream

сливки

SLEEF-KEE

Sugar

сахар

Sah-HahR

Lemon

лимон

LEE-MON

Milk

молоко

M@h-L@h-KO

Hot chocolate

какао

K@h-K@w

Juice

сок

SOK

Orange juice

апельсиновый сок

@h-PEEL-SEE-N@h-VEE SOK

Ice water

вода со льдом

V@h-D@h S@hL-DOM

Mineral water

минеральная вода

MEE-NEE-R@hL-N@h-Y@h V@h-D@h

Ice

лёд

LOD

AT THE BAR

Bartender

Бармен

B@B-M@N

Cocktail

Коктейль

K@K-T@L

With ice

Со льдом

S@L-D@M

Straight

В чистом виде

FCH@S-T@M-V@-D@

With lemon

С лимоном

SL@-M@-N@M

PHRASEMAKER

I would like a glass of...

Дайте мне бокал, пожалуиста...

DĪ-Tẽẽ MNẽẽ Bah-KahL...
Pah-ZHah-Lоо-STah

▶ **champagne**

шампанского

SHah-M-Pah-N-SKah-Vah

▶ **beer**

пива

PẼẼ-Vah

▶ **wine**

вина

VẼẼ-Nah

▶ **red wine**

красного вина

KRah-S-Nah-Vah VẼẼ-Nah

▶ **white wine**

белого вина

Bẽẽ-Lah-Vah VẼẼ-Nah

FAMILIAR FOODS

On the following pages you will
find lists of foods you are familiar
with, along with other information
such as basic utensils and preparation
instructions.

A polite way to get a waiter's or waitress's attention
is to say Можно вас спросить?, which means
May I ask?, followed by your request and thank you.

May I ask...?
Можно вас спросить...?

MŌZH-Nah VahS SPRah-SEET

Please bring me...
Принесите пожалуйста...

PREE-Nĕ-SEE-Tĕĕ
Pah-ZHah-Loo-STah...

Thank you.
Спасибо.

SPah-SEE-Bah

STARTERS

Appetizers

Закуска

Z@h-K@oS-K@h

Bread and butter

Хлеб с маслом

HL@P SM@hS-L@hM

Cheese

Сыр

S@B

Fruit

Фрукты

FR@oK-T@

Salad

Салат

S@h-L@hT

Soup

Суп

S@oP

MEATS

Bacon

Бекон

B⒠-KO͡N

Beef

Говядина

G⒜-V⒠I͡-D⒠-N⒜

Beef steak

Бифштекс

B⒠F-SHT⒠KS

Ham

Ветчина

V⒠T-CH⒠-N⒜

Lamb

Баранина

B⒜-R⒜-N⒠-N⒜

Pork

Свинина

SV⒠-N⒠-N⒜

Veal

Телятина

T⒠-L⒜-T⒠-N⒜

POULTRY

Baked chicken

Запечённая курица

Z@h-P@-CH@-N@h-Y@h K@-B@-TS@h

Grilled chicken

Курица-гриль

K@-B@-TS@h GR@L

Fried chicken

Жареная курица

ZH@h-B@-N@h-Y@h K@-B@-TS@h

Duck

Утка

@T-K@h

Goose

Гусь

G@S

Turkey

Индейка

@N-D@-K@h

SEAFOOD

Fish

Рыба

R̲EE-Bah

Lobster

Омар

ah-Mah R̲

Oysters

Устрицы

oo-STR̲EE-TSEE

Salmon

Сёмга

SEEOM-Gah

Shrimp

Креветки

KR̲EE-VEEeT-KEE

Trout	**Tuna**
Форель	Тунец
Fah-R̲EEeL	Too-NEEeTS

OTHER ENTREES

Sandwich

Бутерброд

Boo-TEER-BRoT

Hot dog

Сосиска

Sah-SEES-Kah

Hamburger

Гамбургер

Gah̄M-Boo̅B-Gĕ̄B

French fries

Жареная картошка

ZHah̄-Bĕ̄-Nah-Yah Kah̄B-TOSH-Kah

Pasta

Макароны

Mah-Kah-BO-NEE

Pizza

Пицца

PEE-TSah

VEGETABLES

Carrots

Морковь

M@B-K©́F

Corn

Кукуруза

K©-K©-R©́-Z@

Mushrooms

Грибы

GR©-BW©́

Onions

Лук

L©K

Potato

Картофель

K@B-T©́-F©L

Rice

Рис

R©S

Tomato

Помидоры

P@-M©-D©́-R©

FRUITS

Apple
Яблоко
Y@B-L@-K@

Banana
Банан
B@-N@N

Grapes
Виноград
V€€-N@-GR@T

Lemon
Лимон
L€€-M@N

Orange
Апельсин
@-P€€L-S€€N

Strawberry	**Watermelon**
Клубника	Арбуз
KL@B-N€€-K@	@R-B@S

DESSERT

Dessert

Десерт

D☺-S☺☺RT

Apple pie

Яблочный пирог

Y☺-BL☺CH-N☺ P☺-R☺K

Cherry pie

Вишнёвый пирог

V☺SH-NY☺-V☺ P☺-R☺K

Pastry

Пирожное

P☺-R☺ZH-N☺-Y☺

Candy

Конфеты

K☺N-F☺☺-T☺

Ice cream

Мороженое

M@h-ROZH-N@h-Y@

Ice cream cone

Мороженое в стаканчике

M@h-ROZH-N@h-Y@
FST@h-K@h-N-CH@E-K@

Chocolate

Шоколадное

SH@h-K@h-L@hD-N@h-Y@

Strawberry

Клубничное

KL@@B-N@E'CH-N@h-Y@

Vanilla

Ванильное

V@h-N@EL-N@h-Y@

CONDIMENTS

Butter
Масло
M@S-L@

Ketchup
Кетчуп
K@-CH@P

Mayonnaise
Майонез
M@@-N@S

Mustard
Горчица
G@B-CH@-TS@

Salt
Соль
S@L

Pepper
Перец
P@-B@TS

Sugar
Сахар
S@-H@B

SETTINGS

A cup
Чашка
CH@SH-K@h

A glass
Стакан
ST@-K@N

A spoon
Ложка
LOZH-K@h

A fork
Вилка
VEEL-K@h

A knife
Нож
NOSH

A plate
Тарелка
T@h-BEEL-K@h

A napkin
Салфетка
S@L-FEET-K@h

HOW DO YOU WANT IT COOKED?

Baked

Печёный

Pⓔ-CHⓄ-Nⓔⓔ

Grilled

Обжаренный на гриле

ⓐB-ZHⓐ-Rⓔ-Nⓔⓔ Nⓐ GRⓔⓔ-Lⓔ

Steamed

Паровой

Pⓐ-Rⓐ-Vⓞⓨ

Fried

Жареный

ZHⓐ-Rⓔ-Nⓔⓔ

Medium

Среднепрожаренный

SRⓔD-Nⓔⓔⓔ-PRⓐ-ZHⓐ-Rⓔ-Nⓔⓔ

Well done

Хорошо прожаренный

Hⓐ-Rⓐ-SHⓄ PRⓐ-ZHⓐ-Rⓔ-Nⓔⓔ

PROBLEMS

I didn't order this. (male speaking)

Я этого не заказывал.

Y@h @́-T@h-V@h N@E-Z@h-K@h́-Z①-V@hL

I didn't order this. (female speaking)

Я этого не заказывала.

Y@h @́-T@h-V@h N@E-Z@h-K@h́-Z①-V@h-L@h

Please check the bill.

Проверьте счёт.

PR@h-V@E@́R-T@E@ SH@T

PRAISE

Thank you for the delicious meal.

Спасибо за вкусную еду.

SP@h-S@E@́-B@h Z@h-FK@@́S-N@@-Y@@
Y@́-D@@́

GETTING AROUND

Getting around in a foreign
country can be an adventure
in itself! Taxi and bus drivers
do not always speak English, so
it is essential to be able to give
simple directions. The words
and phrases in this chapter will
help you get where you're going.

- Metro stations are easily identified by red
  (M) signs and offer the best way to get
  around. There are also public buses and
  taxis.

- In Russia, taxi fees are usually negotiated
  with the driver ahead of time. Do not
  accept rides in cabs that already have a
  rider and in general travel by two.

- It is not a good idea to accept a ride with
  ordinary drivers as Russians traditionally
  do. This works for Russians because they
  speak the language and they know exactly
  where they want to go.

- Have a map or the address you want to
  go to written down in Russian.

- Remember to take a business card from
  your hotel to give to the taxi driver on
  your return.

- Carry your ID with you at all times while
  in Russia.

KEY WORDS

Airport

Аэропорт

@h-@-R@h-PORT

Bus Stop

Автобусная остановка

@hF-TO-B@S-N@h-Y@h

@hS-T@h-NOF-K@h

Car Rental Agency

Аренда машины

@h-R@@N-D@h M@h-SHEE-NEE

Taxi Stand

Стоянка такси

ST@h-Y@hN-K@h T@hK-SEE

Train Station

Вокзал

V@hK-Z@hL

AIR TRAVEL

A one-way ticket, please.

Билет в одну сторону, пожалуйста.

BEE-LEëT VahD-Noo STÖ-Rah-Noo
Pah-ZHah-Loo-STah

A round trip ticket.

Билет туда и обратно.

BEE-LEëT Too-Dah EE-ah-BRahT-Nah

First class

В первом классе

FPëR-VahM KLah-Së

How much do I owe? (male speaking)

Сколько я вам должен?

SKÖL-Kah Yah VahM DÖL-ZHëN

How much do I owe? (female speaking)

Сколько я вам должна?

SKÖL-Kah Yah VahM DahL-ZHNah

The gate

Ворота

Vah-RÖ-Tah

PHRASEMAKER

I would like a seat...(male speaking)

Я бы хотел место...

Y@h BW@ H@h-T@@L M@@S-T@h...

I would like a seat...(female speaking)

Я бы хотела место...

Y@h BW@ H@h-T@@-L@h M@@S-T@h...

▸ **in first class**

в первом классе

FP@@B-V@hM KL@h-S@

▸ **next to the window**

у окна

@-@hK-N@h

▸ **on the aisle**

у прохода

@-PR@h-H@-D@h

▸ **near the exit**

рядом с выходом

R@@h-D@hM SV@-H@h-D@hM

BY BUS

Bus

Автобус

@hF-T@́-B@@S

Where is the bus stop?

Где автобусная остановка?

GDY@̃   @hF-T@́-B@@S-N@h-Y@h

@hS-T@h-N@́F-K@h

Do you go to...?

Вы едите в...?

V@   Y@̃-D@-T@̃@̃   V@h...

What is the fare?

Сколько с меня?

SK@́L-K@h   SM@-NY@h́

Do I need exact change?

Вам нужно без сдачи?

V@hM   N@@́ZH-N@h

B@̃Z-D@h́-CH@

PHRASEMAKER

Which bus goes to...

Какой автобус идёт...

K@h-K@v́ @hF-T@̄-B@@S @̄D-Y@̄T...

▶ **the beach?**

на пляж?

N@h-PL@̄@hSH

▶ **the market?**

на рынок?

N@h-R@̄-N@hK

▶ **the airport?**

в аэропорт?

V@h-@̄-R@h-P@̄RT

▶ **the train station ?**

на вокзал?

N@h-V@hK-Z@h́L

BY CAR

Can you help me?

Вы можете мне помочь?

VEE MÓ-ZHĕ-Tĕĕ MNĕĕ
PĕÞ-MÓCH

My car won't start.

Моя машина не заводится.

MĕÞ-YĕÞ MĕÞ-SHĒĒ-NĕÞ
NĒĒ-ZĕÞ-VÓ-DĕĕT-SYĕÞ

Can you fix it?

Вы можете это починить?

VEE MÓ-ZHĕ-Tĕĕ ĕ-TĕÞ
PĕÞ-CHĒĒ-NĕĕT

What will it cost?

Сколько это будет стоит?

SKÓL-KĕÞ ĕ-TĕÞ Bᴏᴏ-DĕĕT STÓ-ĭT

How long will it take?

Сколько времени это займёт?

SKÓL-KĕÞ VRĕĕĕ-MĕÞ-NĒĒ
ĕ-TĕÞ ZĬ-MĕᴏᴏT

PHRASEMAKER

Please check...

Пожалуйста, проверьте...

P@h-ZH@h-L@o-ST@h PR@h-V@@R-T@@...

▶ **the battery**

батарею

B@h-T@h-R@@-Y@o

▶ **the brakes**

тормоза

T@hR-M@h-Z@h

▶ **the oil**

масло

M@hS-L@h

▶ **the tires**

шины

SH@@-N@@

▶ **the water**

воду

V@-D@o

SUBWAYS AND TRAINS

Where is the train station?

Где вокзал?

GDY@ V@K-Z@L

A one-way ticket, please.

Билет в одну сторону, пожалуйста.

B@-L@T V@D-N@ ST@-R@-N@

P@-ZH@-L@-ST@

A round trip ticket.

Билет туда и обратно.

B@-L@T T@-D@

@-@-BR@T-N@

First class

В первом классе

FP@B-V@M KL@-S@

Second class

Во втором классе

V@-FT@-R@M KL@-S@

What is the fare?

Сколько стоит билет?

SKÓL-K@L STÓ-①T
B@-L@@T

Is this seat taken?

Это место занято?

@-T@ M@@S-T@
Z@-NY@-T@

Do I have to change trains?

Мне нужно делать пересадку?

MN@@ N@ZH-N@
D@-L@T P@-R@-S@D-K@

Where are we?

Где мы?

GDY@ MW@

BY TAXI

Please call a taxi for me.

Закажите мне, пожалуйста, такси.

Z@h-K@h-ZH@-T@ⓔ   MN@ⓔ

P@h-ZH@h-L@-ST@h   T@hK-S@

Are you available?

Вы свободны?

V@   SV@h-B@D-N@

I want to go...

Я хочу поехать...

Y@h   H@h-CH@   P@h-Y@-H@hT...

Stop here, please.

Остановитесь здесь, пожалуйста.

@hS-T@h-N@h-V@-T@S   ZD@S

P@h-ZH@h-L@-ST@h

Please wait.

Подождите, пожалуйста.

P@h-D@hZH-D@-T@ⓔ   P@h-ZH@h-L@-ST@h

How much do I owe?

Сколько с меня?

SK@L-K@h   SM@-NY@h

PHRASEMAKER

The simplest way to get to
where you want to go is to
name the destination and say **please**.

▶ **This address...**

По этому адресу...

P@h-@-T@h-M@o @hD-R@-S@o...

Have someone at your hotel write down the address
for you in Russian.

▶ **This hotel...**

В гостиницу...

VG@hS-T@-N@-TS@o...

▶ **Airport...**

В аэропорт...

V@h-@-R@h-P@RT...

▶ **Subway station...**

На станцию метро...

N@h-ST@hN-TS@-Y@o M@-TR@...

...please.

...пожалуйста.

...P@h-ZH@h-L@o-ST@h

SHOPPING

Whether you plan a major shopping spree or just need to purchase some basic necessities, the following information is useful.

- Upon arriving in Russia, tourists must fill out a customs declaration form. Keep this with you until you leave as it lists your personal items.

- Visitors to Russia will enjoy shopping, particularly in Moscow and St. Petersburg, where shops cater to tourists. There are several souvenir shops, department stores and small outdoor stands. You can also find a wide array of arts and antiques.

- When purchasing items, ask the shop keeper for a certificate that shows that your purchases have been paid by hard currency.

- Allow extra time for shopping as prices vary from shop to shop. Payment is expected in rubles.

- Shopping hours in Russia are Monday through Saturday 9:00 AM to 7:00 PM. Many food shops remain open on Sundays.

KEY WORDS

Credit card

Кредитная карточка

KREE-DEET-Nah-Yah Kah'R-TahCH-Kah

Money

Деньги

DEEĕ'N-GEE

Receipt

Квитанция

KVEE-Tah'N-TSEE-Yah

Sale

Распродажа

Rah'S-PRah-Dah'-ZHah

Store

Магазин

Mah-Gah-ZEE'N

Traveler's checks

Дорожные чеки

Dah-RO'ZH-NEE-Yĕ CHĕ'-KEE

USEFUL PHRASES

Do you sell...?

Вы продаёте...?

VⒺ PⓇⓐ-Dⓐ-YⓄ́-TⓔⒺ...

Do you have...?

У вас есть...?

ⓄⓄ-Vⓐ S Yⓔ́ST...

I want to buy...(male speaking)

Я хотел бы купить...

Yⓐ Hⓐ-TⓔⒺ́L BWⒺ KⓄⓄ-PⓔⒺ́T...

I want to buy...(female speaking)

Я хотела бы купить...

Yⓐ Hⓐ-TⓔⒺ́-Lⓐ BWⒺ KⓄⓄ-PⓔⒺ́T...

How much?

Сколько стоит?

SKⓄ́L-Kⓐ STⓄ́-ⓘT

When do the shops open?

Когда открываются магазины?

KⓐG-Dⓐ́ ⓐT-KⓇⒺ-Vⓐ́-YⓄⓄ-TSⓐ
Mⓐ-Gⓐ-ZⒺ́-NⒺ

No, thank you.

Нет, спасибо.

NⒺⒺT SPⓐ-SⒺⒺ-Bⓐ

I´m just looking.

Я просто смотрю.

Yⓐ PRⓄS-Tⓐ SMⓐ-TRⓄⓄ

Is it very expensive?

Это очень дорого?

Ⓔ-Tⓐ Ⓞ-CHⒺN DⓄ-Rⓐ-Gⓐ

Can't you give me a discount?

Вы можете дать скидку?

VⒺⒺ MⓄ-ZHⒺ-TⒺⒺ
Dⓐ T SKⒺⒺT-KⓄⓄ

I'll take it.

Я возьму это.

Yⓐ VⓐZ-MⓄⓄ Ⓔ-Tⓐ

I'd like a receipt, please.

Даите мне чек, пожалуйста.

DⓄⒻ-TⒺ MNⒺⒺ
CHⒺⒺK Pⓐ-ZHⓐ-LⓄⓄ-STⓐ

SHOPS AND SERVICES

Bakery

Булочная

B⊚́-L⒜CH-N⒜-Y⒜

Bank	**Hair salon / Barbershop**
Банк	Парикмахерская
B⒜NK	P⒜-R⒠K-M⒜́-H⒠R-SK⒜-Y⒜

Jewelry store

Ювелирный

Y⒪⒪-V⒠́-L⒠́R-N⒠

Bookstore	**News stand**
Книжный магазин	Газетный киоск
KN⒠́ZH-N⒠	G⒜-Z⒠́⒠́T-N⒠
M⒜-G⒜-Z⒠́N	K⒠-⊙́SK

Camera shop

Фотомагазин

F⊙-T⒜-M⒜-G⒜-Z⒠́N

Pharmacy

Аптека

⒜P-T⒠⒠́-K⒜

SHOPPING LIST

On the following pages you will find some common items you may need to purchase on your trip.

Aspirin

Аспирин

@S-P㋴-R㋴N

Cigarettes

Сигареты

S㋴-G@-R㋴㋴-T①

Deodorant

Дезодорант

D㋴-Z@-D@-R@NT

Dress

Платье

PL@-T㋴㋴

Film (camera)

Плёнка

PL㋴①N-K@

Perfume

Духи

D⊙⊙-H🅴🅴

Razor blade

Лезвие

L🅴🅴Z-V🅴🅴-Y🅴

Shampoo

Шампунь

SH🅰M-P⊙⊙N

Shaving cream

Крем для бритья

KR🅴M DL🅰 BR🅴🅴-T🅴🅰

Shirt

Рубашка

R⊙⊙-B🅰SH-K🅰

Sunglasses

Солнечные очки

S⊙L-N🅴🅴CH-N🅴🅴-Y🅴   🅰CH-K🅴🅴

Suntan oil

Крем для загара

KR(ĕ)M DLY@h Z@h-G@h-R@h

Toothbrushes

Зубные шётки

Z(oo)B-N(Ē)-Y(ē) SH(o)T-K(ee)

Toothpaste

Зубная паста

Z(oo)B-N@h-Y@h P@hS-T@h

Water (bottled)

Бутылка воды

B(oo)-T(i)L-K@h V@h-D(ee)

Water (mineral)

Минеральная вода

M(ee)-N(ĕ)-R@hL-N@h-Y@h V@h-D@h

ESSENTIAL SERVICES

THE BANK

As a traveler in a foreign country your primary contact with banks will be to exchange money.

- The official Russian currency is the ruble (RUB) divided into 100 kopeks. It is important to take good condition US dollars or Euro notes to change.

- Banks are usually open from Mondays to Fridays between 9:30 AM and 5:30 PM.

- Currency can be changed at banks, currency exchange booths, and hotels.

- ATMs are widely available in major cities. Check with your bank to see if your card is accepted and get exact locations.

- Cash advances on credit cards can be handled at the bank, but may be subject to a higher commission.

- Most large hotels and tourist areas accept major credit cards, however, almost everything has to be paid for in rubles.

KEY WORDS

Bank

Банк

B@hNK

Exchange bureau

Обмен валюты

@hB-M@@N V@h-L@@-T@

Money

Деньги

D@@N-G@

Money order

Денежный чек

D@@-N@ZH-N@ CH@K

Traveler's check

Дорожный чек

D@h-R@ZH-N@ CH@K

USEFUL PHRASES

Where is the bank?

Где банк?

GDYⓔ BⓐNK

At what time does the bank open?

Во сколько открывается банк?

Vⓐ-SKOֺL-Kⓐ
ⓐT-KRⒺⒺ-Vⓐ-Yⓔ-TSⓐ BⓐNK

Where is the exchange office?

Где обмен валюты?

GDYⓔ ⓐB-MⒺⓔN Vⓐ-Lⓞⓞ-Tⓘ

At what time does the exchange office open?

Во сколько открывается обмен валюты?

Vⓐ SKOֺL-Kⓐ ⓐT-KRⒺⒺ-Vⓐ-Yⓔ-TSⓐ
ⓐB-MⒺⓔN Vⓐ-Lⓞⓞ-Tⓘ

Can I change dollars here?

Можно обменять доллары здесь?

MOֺZH-Nⓐ ⓐB-MⒺ-NYⓐT
DOֺ-Lⓐ-RⒺⒺ ZDⓔS

What is the exchange rate?

Какой курс валюты сейчас?

K@h-K@y K@@RS
V@h-L@@-T① S@-CH@h'S

I would like large bills.

Мне нужны крупные купюры.

MN@@ N@@ZH-N@
KR@@P-N@-Y@ K@@-P@@@-R@

I would like small bills.

Мне нужны мелкие купюры.

MN@@ N@@ZH-N@
M@@L-K@-Y@ K@@-P@@@-R@

I need change.

Мне нужна мелочь.

MN@@ N@@ZH-N@h
M@@-L@hCH

Do you have an ATM?

У вас есть банкомат?

@@-V@hS Y@ST
B@hN-K@h-M@h'T

POST OFFICE

If you are planning on sending letters and postcards, be sure to send them early so that you don't arrive home before they do.

KEY WORDS

Air mail

Авиапочта

@h-V@-@h-P@CH-T@h

Letter

Письмо

P@S-M@

Post office

Почта

P@CH-T@h

Postcard

Открытка

@T-K@@T-K@h

Stamp

Марка

M@B-K@h

USEFUL PHRASES

Where is the post office?

Где почта?

GDYⓔ PÓCH-Tⓐⓗ

What time does the post office open?

Во сколько почта открывается?

Vⓐⓗ SKÓL-Kⓐⓗ PÓCH-Tⓐⓗ
ⓐⓗT-KRⒺⒺ-Vⓐⓗ-Yⓔ-TSⓐⓗ

I need...

Мне надо...

MNⒺⓔ Nⓐⓗ-Dⓐⓗ...

I need stamps.

Мне нужны марки.

MNⒺⓔ NⓄⓄZH-NⒺⒺ MⓐⓗR-KⒺⒺ

I need envelopes.

Мне нужны конверты.

MNⒺⓔ NⓄⓄZH-NⒺⒺ KⓐⓗN-VⒺⓔR-Tⓘ

I need a pen.

Мне нужна ручка.

MNⒺⓔ NⓄⓄZH-Nⓐⓗ RⓄⓄCH-Kⓐⓗ

TELEPHONE

Placing phone calls in Russia can be a test of will and stamina! Besides the obvious language barriers, service can vary greatly from one city to the next.

- You should be able to use your cell phone in Russia if your company has an agreement with local operators, but the roaming charges can be high.

- You can purchase a local SIM card and pay-as-you-go set for a reasonable price and it will include a Russian phone number.

- Prepaid IP phone cards can be purchased at telecom shops or at banks.

- Laptops are allowed to be brought into Russia for personal use.

- Internet access is available at post-offices in big cities for a fee.

KEY WORDS

Information

Информация

ⒺN-FⓐⓇ-Mⓐ́-TSⒺ-Yⓐ

Long distance (call)

Междугородний

Mⓔ́ZH-Dⓞⓞ-Gⓐ-RⓄ́D-NⒺ

Operator

Телефонистка

Tⓔ-Lⓔ̌-Fⓐ-NⒺ́ST-Kⓐ

Phone book

Телефонная книга

Tⓔ-Lⓔ̌-FⓄ́-Nⓐ-Yⓐ KNⒺ́-Gⓐ

Public telephone

Телефонный автомат

Tⓔ-Lⓔ̌-FⓄ́-NⒺ ⓐF-Tⓐ-Mⓐ́T

Telephone

Телефон

Tⓔ-Lⓔ̌-FⓄ́N

USEFUL PHRASES

Where is the telephone?

Где телефон?

GDY☯ T☯-L☯-FⓄN

Where is the public telephone?

Где Телефонный автомат?

GDY☯ T☯-L☯-FⓄ-N☞ ⓐF-Tⓐh-Mⓐh'T

May I use your telephone?

Можно позвонить от вас?

MⓄZH-Nⓐh Pⓐh Z-Vⓐh-N☞'T
ⓐhT-Vⓐh'S

Operator, I don't speak Russian.

Телефонистка, я не говорю по-русски.

T☯-L☯-Fⓐh-N☞'ST-Kⓐh
Yⓐh N☞ Gⓐh-Vⓐh-RⓄⓄ
Pⓐh-RⓄⓄ'S-K☞

I want to call this number...

Я хочу позвонить по этому номеру...

Yah Hah-CHoo PahZ-Vah-NEET
Pah-ě-Tah-Moo NO-Mě-Roo...

1	2	3
один	два	три
ah-DEEN	DVah	TREE

4	5	6
четыре	пять	шесть
CHEE-TEE-Rě	PaT	SHěST

7	8	9
семь	восемь	девять
SěěM	VO-SěěM	Děě-VěT

★	0	#
	ноль	
	NOL	

SIGHTSEEING AND ENTERTAINMENT

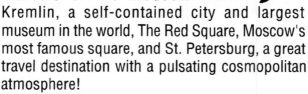

Russia is a country with a very rich history and culture. It is the largest country on earth. Discover Russia through the architectural marvels of the Moscow Kremlin, a self-contained city and largest museum in the world, The Red Square, Moscow's most famous square, and St. Petersburg, a great travel destination with a pulsating cosmopolitan atmosphere!

- The **Moscow Kremlin**, one of the largest museums in the world, is a city within itself. It contains palaces, churches, Russian Tsar treasures and has observed the most tragic and famous of events.

- **Red Square** was founded in 1147 and is surrounded by Lobnoye Mesto, the Mausoleum and Saint Basil's Cathedral. Krasnaya Ploschad is the Russian name for this famous square.

KEY WORDS

Admission

Вход

FH◎T

Map

Карта

K⏣R-T⏣

Reservation

Бронирование

BR⏣-NEE-R⏣-V⏣-NEEê

Ticket

Билет

BEE-Lêêê'T

Tour

Тур

TOOR

Tour guide

Гид

GEED

USEFUL PHRASES

Where is the tourist agency?

Где туристическое агенство?

GDYⓔ
Tⓞⓞ-RⓔⓔS-Tⓔⓔ-CHⓔⓔS-Kⓐⓗ-Yⓔ
ⓐⓗ-GⓔNST-Vⓐⓗ

Where do I buy a ticket?

Где я могу купить билет?

GDYⓔ Yⓐⓗ Mⓐⓗ-Gⓞⓞ
Kⓞⓞ-PⓔⓔT Bⓔⓔ-LⓔⓔⓔT

How much?

Сколько это стоит?

SKⓞL-Kⓐⓗ ⓔ-Tⓐⓗ STⓞ-ⓞT

How long?

Как долго?

KⓐⓗK DⓞL-Gⓐⓗ

When?
Когда?

KⓐⓗG-Dⓐⓗ

Where?
Где?
GDYⓔ

Do I need reservations?

Мне нужно бронировать билеты?

MNⒺⓔ NⓄⓄZH-Nⓐⓗ
BRⓐⓗ-NⒺⒺ-Rⓐⓗ-VⓐⓗT BⒺⒺ-LⒺⓔ-Tⓘ

Does the guide speak English?

Гид говорит по-английски?

GⒺⒺD Gⓐⓗ-Vⓐⓗ-RⒺⒺT
Pⓐⓗ-ⓐⓗN-GLⒺⒺ-SKⒺⒺ

How much do children pay?

Сколько стоит детский билет?

SKⓄL-Kⓐⓗ STⓄ-ⓘT
DⒺⒺT-SKⒺⒺ BⒺⒺ-LⒺⓔT

I need your help.

Мне нужна ваша помощь.

MNⒺⓔ NⓄⓄZH-Nⓐⓗ Vⓐⓗ-SHⓐⓗ
PⓄ-MⓐⓗSHCH

Thank you.

Спасибо.

SPⓐⓗ-SⒺⒺ-Bⓐⓗ

PHRASEMAKER

May I invite you to...

Можно вас пригласить...

MⓄZH-Nⓐ VⓐS PRⒺ-GLⓐ-SⒺT...

▸ **a concert?**
на концерт?
Nⓐ-Kⓐ-TSⒺRT

▸ **to dance?**
на танец?
Nⓐ-Tⓐ-NⒺTS

▸ **to dinner?**
на ужин?
Nⓐ-ⓄⓄ-ZHⒺN

▸ **to the movies?**
в кино?
FKⒺ-NⓄ

▸ **the theatre?**
в театр?
FTⒺ-ⓐ-TR

St. Petersburg is notably described as the most beautiful
European city. It hosts a brand of its own magnificent history
and exciting culture and has been depicted as the Venice
of the North.

PHRASEMAKER

Where can I find...

Я ищу́...

Y@h @-SHCH@...

▶ **a health club?**

фитнес-клуб

F@T-N@S KL@P

▶ **a swimming pool?**

бассейн

B@-S@@N

▶ **a tennis court?**

теннисный корт

T@-N@S-N@ K@RT

▶ **a golf course?**

площадку для гольфа

PL@-SHCH@T-K@ DLY@ G@L-F@

HEALTH

Hopefully you will not need medical attention on your trip. If you do, it is important to communicate basic information regarding your condition.

- Travelers to Russia are urged to obtain overseas medical insurance which includes hospitalization and medical evacuation.

- If you take prescription medicine, carry your prescription with you.

- Take a small first-aid kit with you. You may want to include basic cold, anti-diarrhea, and allergy medications. However, you should be able to find most items, like aspirin, locally.

- It is important to drink bottled water as well as using it for brushing your teeth.

- Hospitals usually close on weekends but emergency clinics are open seven days a week and in most cases require fees be paid in advance.

KEY WORDS

Ambulance

Скорая помощь

SKŎ-Bah-Yah PŎ-Mah SH

Dentist

Дантист

DahN-TEE'ST

Doctor

Врач

VBahCH

Hospital

Больница

BahL-NEE-TSah

Prescription

Рецепт от врача

Bĕ-TSĕ'PT ahT-VBah-CHah

USEFUL PHRASES

I am sick. (male speaking)

Я болен.

Yⓐh BŌ´-LⓔⓔN

I am sick. (female speaking)

Я больна.

Yⓐh Bⓐh L-Nⓐh´

I need a doctor.

Мне нужен врач.

MNYⓔ Nⓞⓞ´-ZHⓔN VRⓐhCH

It's an emergency!

Это срочно!

ⓔ´-Tⓐh SRŌCH-Nⓐh

Call an ambulance!

Вызовите скорую помощь!

Vⓔⓔ-Zⓐh-Vⓔⓔ´-Tⓔⓔ

SKŌ´-Rⓞⓞ-Yⓞⓞ PŌ´-MⓐhSHCH

I'm allergic to...

У меня аллергия на...

ⓞⓞ-ⓂⒺⒺ-NYⓐ ⓐ-LⒺR-GⒺⒺ-Yⓐ Nⓐ...

I'm pregnant.

Я беременна.

Yⓐ BⒺⒺ-RⒺⒺ-MⒺN-Nⓐ

I'm diabetic.

У меня диабет.

ⓞⓞ-ⓂⒺⒺ-NYⓐ DⒺⒺ-ⓐ-BⒺT

I have a heart condition.

У меня болезнь сердца.

ⓞⓞ-ⓂⒺⒺ-NYⓐ Bⓐ-LⒶⒺ-ZⒺN
SⒺR-TSⓐ

I have high blood pressure.

У меня повышенное давление.

ⓞⓞ-ⓂⒺⒺ-NYⓐ Pⓐ-VⒺⒺ-SHⒺ-Nⓐ-YⒺ
DⓐV-LⒺ-NⒺⒺ-YⒺ

I have low blood pressure.

У меня пониженное давление.

ⓞⓞ-ⓂⒺⒺ-NYⓐ Pⓐ-NⒺⒺ-ZHⒺ-Nⓐ-YⒺ
DⓐV-LⒺⒺ-NⒺⒺ-YⒺ

PHRASEMAKER

I need...

Мне нужен...

MN@@@ N@@-ZH@N...

▶ **a doctor**

врач

VR@CH

▶ **a dentist**

зубной врач

Z@@B-N@Y VR@CH

▶ **an optician**

оптик

@P-T@@K

I need a nurse.

Мне нужна медсестра.

MN@@@ N@@ZH-N@h M@T-S@@S-TR@h

I need a pharmacy.

Мне нужна аптека.

MN@@@ N@@ZH-N@h @hP-T@-K@h

PHRASEMAKER
(AT THE PHARMACY)

Do you have...

У вас есть...

@-V@S Y@ST...

▸ **aspirin?**

аспирин?

@S-P@-R@N

▸ **Band-Aids?**

пластыри?

PL@S-T@-R@

▸ **cough syrup?**

микстура от кашля?

M@K-ST@-R@ @T-K@SH-L@@

▸ **ear drops?**

ушные капли?

@SH-N@-Y@ K@-PL@

▸ **eye drops?**

глазые капли?

GL@Z-N@-Y@ K@-PL@

BUSINESS TRAVEL

It is important to show appreciation and interest in another person's language and culture, particularly when doing business. A few well-pronounced phrases can make a great impression.

- Business cards are essential. If possible, ensure that one side is printed in Russian and one side in English.

- Business dress is conservative and good shoes are important. Men should not remove their jackets without asking.

- The head of the organization will usually begin with introductions in order of importance.

- It is important to give a firm hand shake when both greeting and leaving your Russian partners.

- Initially meetings will begin with some small talk, before moving on to business discussion.

- Rules of business follow closely to a Russian proverb, "Don't hurry to reply, but hurry to listen".

- Computers: It is a good idea to bring a converter if you want to work online.

KEY WORDS

Appointment (business)

Встреча

FSTR**ё**-CH**ah**

Business card

Визитная карточка

V**EE**-Z**EE**T-N**ah**-Y**ah** K**ah**R-T**ah**CH-K**ah**

Meeting

Собрание

S**ah**-BR**ah**-N**EE**-Y**ё**

Marketing department

Отдел по рекламе

ahT-D**ёё**L P**ah**-R**ё**-KL**ah**-M**ёё**

Office	**Presentation**
Офис	Презентация
O-F**i**S	PR**EE**-Z**ё**N-T**ah**-TS**EE**ah

Telephone

Телефон

T**ё**-L**ё**-F**O**N

USEFUL PHRASES

I have an appointment.

У меня назначена встреча.

ⓞⓞ-Mⓔⓔ-NYⓐⓗ NⓐⓗZ-Nⓐⓗ-CHⓔ-Nⓐⓗ
FSTBⓔ-CHⓐⓗ

My name is...(your name). **Pleased to meet you.**

Меня зовут...(ваше имя). Очень приятно
познакомиться.

Mⓔⓔ-NYⓐⓗ Zⓐⓗ-VⓞⓞT...(your name).
ⓞ-CHⓔⓔN PBⓔⓔ-YⓐⓗT-Nⓐⓗ
PⓐⓗZ-Nⓐⓗ-Kⓞ-Mⓔⓔ-TSⓐⓗ

Here is my card.

Вот моя визитка.

VⓞT Mⓐⓗ-Yⓐⓗ Vⓔⓔ-ZⓔⓔT-Kⓐⓗ

I need an interpreter.

Мне нужен переводчик.

MNⓔⓔⓔ Nⓞⓞ-ZHⓔN
Pⓔ-Bⓔ-VⓞD-CHⓞK

Can you write your address for me?

Не могли бы вы написать свой адрес?

N㊙㊙ M@G-L㊙ BW㊙ V㊙
N@-P㊙-S@T SV㊛ @-DR㊙S

Can you write your phone number?

Не могли бы вы написать свой
номер телефона?

N㊙㊙ M@G-L㊙ BW㊙ V㊙
N@-P㊙-S@T SV㊛ N㊒-M㊙B
T㊙-L㊙-F㊒-N@

This is my phone number.

Вот мой номер телефона.

V㊒T M㊛ N㊒-M㊙B
T㊙-L㊙-F㊒-N@

His / Her name is...

Его / её зовут...

Y㊙-V㊒ / Y㊙-Y㊒ Z@-V㊛T...

Good-bye

До свидания

D@-SV㊙-D@-NY@

PHRASEMAKER

I need...

Мне нужен...

MN@@ N@@-ZH@N...

▶ **a computer**

компьютер

K@M-PY@@-T@R

▶ **a copy machine**

ксерокс

KS@-R@KS

▶ **a fax or fax machine**

факс

F@KS

▶ **a lawyer**

адвокат

@D-V@-K@T

▶ **a notary**

нотариус

N@-T@-R@@-@@S

I need a conference room.

Мне нужна комната дла конференций.

MNⓔⓔ NⓄⓄZH-Nⓐ⒣ KⓄ́M-Nⓐ⒣-Tⓐ⒣
DLYⓐ⒣ Kⓐ⒣N-Fⓔⓔ-Rⓔ́N-TSⓔⓔ

I need a pen.

Мне нужна ручка.

MNⓔⓔ NⓄⓄZH-Nⓐ⒣ RⓄⓄ́CH-Kⓐ⒣

I need stamps.

Мне нужны марки.

MNⓔⓔ NⓄⓄZH-Nⓘ Mⓐ⒣́R-Kⓔⓔ

I need stationery.

Мне нужны канцелярские
принадлежности.

MNⓔⓔ NⓄⓄZH-Nⓘ
Kⓐ⒣N-TSⓔ́-LYⓐ⒣́R-SKⓔⓔ-Yⓔ́
PRⓔⓔ-Nⓐ⒣D-Lⓔ́ZH-Nⓐ⒣S-Tⓔⓔ

I need typing paper.

Мне нужна бумага для печати.

MNⓔⓔ NⓄⓄZH-Nⓐ⒣ BⓄⓄ-Mⓐ⒣́-Gⓐ⒣
DLYⓐ⒣ Pⓔⓔ-CHⓐ⒣́-Tⓔⓔ

GENERAL INFORMATION

SEASONS

Spring

Весна

VēS-Nah

Summer

Лето

Lēē-Tah

Autumn

Осень

Ō-SēēN

Winter

Зима

ZEE-Mah

THE DAYS

Monday
Понедельник
Pᵃʰ-NEE-DᵒᵒᵉL-NEEK

Tuesday
Вторник
FTOᵣB-NEEK

Wednesday
Среда
SBᵉᵉ-Dᵃʰ

Thursday
Четверг
CHᵉᵗT-VᵉᵉᵉᵣBK

Friday
Пятница
PᵉᵉᵃT-NEE-TSᵃʰ

Saturday
Суббота
Sᵒᵒ-BOᵗ-Tᵃʰ

Sunday
Воскресенье
VᵃʰS-KBᵉᵉ-Sᵉᵉᵉ-Nᵉᵉᵉ

THE MONTHS

January	**February**
Январь	Февраль
Y@N-V@R	F@V-R@L

March	**April**
Март	Апрель
M@RT	@-PR@L

May	**June**
Май	Июнь
M①	@-Y@N

July	**August**
Июль	Август
@-Y@L	@V-G@ST

September	**October**
Сентябрь	Октябрь
S@N-T@@-BR	@K-T@@-BR

November	**December**
Ноябрь	Декабрь
N@-Y@-BR	D@-K@-BR

COLORS

Black
Чёрный
CHⓔⓄB-Nⓔⓔ

White
Белый
Bⓔⓔⓔ-Lⓔⓔ

Blue
Синий
Sⓔⓔ-Nⓔⓔ

Brown
Коричневый
Kⓐⓗ-BⓔⓔCH-Nⓔ-Vⓔⓔ

Gray
Серый
Sⓔ-Bⓔⓔ

Gold
Золотой
Zⓐⓗ-Lⓐⓗ-TⓄⓨ

Orange
Оранжевый
ⓐⓗ-BⓐⓗN-ZHⓔ-Vⓔⓔ

Yellow
Жёлтый
ZHⓄL-Tⓔⓔ

Red
Красный
KBⓐⓗS-Nⓔⓔ

Green
Зелёный
Zⓔ-LⓄ-Nⓔⓔ

Pink
Розовый
BⓄ-Zⓐⓗ-Vⓔⓔ

Purple
Фиолетовый
Fⓔⓔⓐⓗ-Lⓔⓔⓔ-Tⓐⓗ-Vⓔⓔ

NUMBERS

0	**1**	**2**
ноль	один	два
NOL	ah-DEEN	DVah

3	**4**	**5**	**6**
три	четыре	пять	шесть
TREE	CHē-TEE-Rē	PahT	SHēST

7	**8**	**9**	**10**
сем	восемь	девять	десять
SēēM	VO-SēēM	Dēē-Vēt	Dēē-Sēt

11	**12**
одиннадцать	двенадцать
ah-DEE-Nah-TSēT	DVEE-Nah-TSēT

13	**14**
тринадцать	четырнадцать
TREE-Nah-TSēT	CHEE-TēēR-Nah-TSēT

15	**16**
пятнадцать	шестнадцать
PahT-Nah-TSēT	SHēST-Nah-TSēT

17	**18**
семнадцать	восемнадцать
SēēM-Nah-TSēT	Vah-SēēM-Nah-TSēT

19	20
девятнадцать	двадцать
DEE-VÊT-NаĥTSÊT	DVаĥ-TSÊT

30	40
тридцать	сорок
TRÊD-SÊT	SÖ-RаĥK

50	60
пятьдесят	шестьдесят
PEE-DEE-SYаĥT	SHEEZ-DEE-SYаĥT

70	80
семьдесят	восемьдесят
SЕÊM-DEE-SÊT	VÖ-SEEM-DEE-SÊT

90	100
девяносто	сто
DÊ-VEE-NÖS-Tаĥ	STÖ

1,000	1,000,000
тысяча	миллион
TÖ-SEE-CHаĥ	MEE-LEE-ÖN

DICTIONARY

Each English entry is followed
by the Russian word in the
Cyrillic Alphabet followed
by the EPLS Vowel Symbol
System. Masculine words will
be followed by (m), feminine (f).

A

a lot много MNŌ-G@

able (to be) мочь MŌCH

accident авария @-V@-B@-Y@

accommodation жильё ZH@-LYŌ

account счёт SHCH@T

address адрес @-DB@S

admission (entrance) вход FH@T

afraid (to be) бояться B@-Y@-TS@

after после P@-SL@@

afternoon день D@@N

agency агенство @-G@@N-STV@

air-conditioning кондиционер
 K@N-D@-TS@-@-N@@B

aircraft самолёт S@-M@-LY@T

airline авиалиния @-V@-@-L@-N@@

airport аэропорт @-@-B@-P@BT

aisle проход PR@-HOT

all всё FSYO

almost почти P@CH-T@

alone (m) один @-D@@N

alone (f) одна @D-N@

also также T@G-ZH@

always всегда FS@G-D@

ambulance скорая помощь
SKO-R@-Y@ PO-M@SHCH

American (m) (nationality) американец
@-M@-R@-K@-N@@TS

American (f) (nationality) американка
@-M@-R@-K@N-K@

and и @

another другой DR@-GOY

anything что-либо SHTO-L@-B@

apartment квартира KV@R-T@-R@

appetizers закуска Z@-K@S-K@

apple яблоко Y@B-L@-K@

appointment встреча FSTR@-CH@

April апрель @-PR@L

arrival прибытие PR@-B@-T@-Y@

ashtray пепельница P@-P@L-N@-TS@

aspirin аспирин ⓐS-PⒺ-RⒺN

attention внимание VNⒺ-MⓐN-Ⓔ-YⒺ

August август ⓐV-GⓄST

Australia Австралия ⓐF-STRⓐ-LⒺ-Yⓐ

Australian (person) Австралиец
ⓐF-STRⓐ-LⒺ-YⒺTS

author автор ⓐF-TⓐR

automobile машина Mⓐ-SHⒺ-Nⓐ

autumn осень Ⓞ-SⒺⒺN

avenue проспект PRⓐS-PⒺKT

awful ужасно ⓄⓄ-ZHⓐ-SNⓐ

B

baby ребёнок RⒺ-BYⓄ-NⓐK

babysitter няня NⒺⓐ-NⒺⓐ

bacon бекон BⒺ-KⓄN

bad плохой PLⓐ-HⓄY

bag сумка SⓄⓄM-Kⓐ

baggage багаж Bⓐ-GⓐSH

baked печёный PⒺ-CHⓄ-NⒺ

bakery булочная BⓄⓄ-LⓐCH-Nⓐ-Yⓐ

banana банан Bⓐ-NⓐN

Band-Aid пластырь PLⓐ-STⓄR

bank банк BⓐNK

barbershop парикмахерская
P@h-B@K-M@h-H@R-SK@h-Y@h

bartender бармен B@B-M@N

bath ванна V@h-N@h

bathing suit купальник K@-P@L-N@K

bathroom туалет T@@h-L@@T

battery батарея B@h-T@h-B@@-Y@h

beach пляж PL@@h'ZH

beautiful красивый KR@h-S@@-V@

beauty shop салон S@h-L@N

bed постель P@h-ST@@L

beef говядина G@h-V@@h'-D@@-N@h

beer пиво P@@'-V@h

bellman швейцар SHV@@-TS@B

belt ремень B@-M@@N

big большой B@hL-SH@

bill чек CH@K

black чёрный CH@@B-N@

blanket одеяло @h-D@@-Y@h-L@h

blue синий S@@-N@

boat лодка L@T-K@h

book книга KN@@-G@h

bookstore   книжный магазин
  KNEEZH-NEE M@h-G@h-ZEEN

border   граница   GR@h-NEE-TS@h

boy   мальчик   M@hL-CHEEK

bracelet   браслет   BR@h-SLEET

brakes   тормоза   TOB-M@h-Z@h

bread   хлеб   HLEEP

breakfast   завтрак   Z@hF-TR@hK

broiled   жареный   ZH@h-REE-NEE

brother   брат   BR@hT

brown   коричневый   K@h-REECH-NEE-VEE

brush   щётка   SHCHOT-K@h

building   здание   ZD@h-NEE-YE

bus   автобус   @hF-TO-B@@S

bus station   автовокзал   @hF-T@h-V@hG-Z@hL

bus stop   автобусная остановка
  @hF-TO-B@@S-N@h-Y@h   @hS-T@h-NOF-K@h

business   бизнес   BEEZ-NES

butter   масло   M@hS-L@h

buy (to)   купить   K@@-PEET

C

cab   такси   T@hK-SEE

call (to)   звонить   ZV@h-NEET

camera фотоаппарат FO-Tah-ah-Pah-Raht

Canada Канада Kah-Nah-Dah

Canadian (person) Канадец Kah-Nah-DeTS

candy конфета Kahn-Fee-Tah

car машина Mah-SHee-Nah

carrot морковь Mahb-KOF

castle замок Zah-Mahk

cathedral собор Sah-BOB

celebration празднование PRahZ-Nah-Vah-Nee

center центр TSeNTR

cereal (cold) крупа KRoo-Pah

chair стул STooL

champagne шампанское SHahM-Pahn-SKah-Ye

change (to) изменить eeZ-Mee-Neet

change (to) (money) разменять Rahz-Mee-Neet

cheap дешёвый Dee-SHO-Vee

check (restaurant bill) чек CHeK

cheers! за здоровье! Zah-ZDah-RO-Vee

cheese сыр SeeR

chicken курица Koo-Ree-TSah

child ребёнок Ree-Bee0-Nahk

chocolate шоколад SHah-Kah-LahD

church церковь TSeR-Kahf

cigar   сигара   SEE-Gah-Rah

cigarette   сигарета   SEE-Gah-REE-Tah

city   город   GO-Rah T

clean   чистый   CHEE-STEE

close (to)   закрыть   Zah-KREET

closed   закрыто   Zah-KREE-Tah

clothes   одежда   ah-DEEZH-Dah

cocktail   коктейль   Kah K-TAL

coffee   кофе   KO-FE

cold (temperture)   холодный   Hah-LOD-NEE

comb   расчёска   Rah-SHCHO-SKah

company   фирма   FEEB-Mah

computer   компьютер   Kah M-PEEO-TER

concert   концерт   Kah N-TSERT

conference   конференция   Kah N-FE-REEN-TSEEah

congratulations   поздравляю   PahZ-DRah V-LEEah-Yoo

copy machine   ксерокс   KSEE-RahKS

corn   кукуруза   Koo-Koo-ROO-Zah

cough syrup   микстура от кашля
MEEK-STOO-Rah   ah T-Kah SH-LEEah

cover charge   входной билет
VHah D-NoV   BEE-LEET

crab   краб   KBahP

cream сливки SLEE'F-KEE

credit card кредитная карточа
KREE-DEET-Nah-Yah Kah'B-Tah'CH-Kah

cup чашка CHah'SH-Kah

customs таможня Tah-MOZH-Neeah

D

dance (to) танцевать Tah-N-TSee-Vah'T

dangerous опасный ah-Pah'S-NEE

date (calendar) число CHEE-SLO

day день DEE'EN

December декабрь DEE-Kah'BB

delicious вкусный FKoo'S-NEE

delighted (m) рад Bah'T

delighted (f) рада Bah'-Dah

dentist дантист Dah'N-TEE'ST

deodorant дезодорант DEE-Zah-Dah-Bah'NT

department отдел ah'T-DEE'EL

departure отъезд ah'T-YEE'ST

dessert десерт DEE-SEE'E'BT

detour объезд ah'B-YEE'ZD

diabetic диабетик DEE-ah-BEE'E'-TEEK

diarrhea понос Pah'-NO'S

dictionary   словарь   SL@h-V@hR

dinner   ужин   @-ZH@N

dining room   столовая   ST@h-L@-V@h-Y@h

direction   направление   N@h-PR@h-VL@-N@-Y@

dirty   грязный   GBY@h-ZN@

disabled   инвалид   @N-V@h-L@T

discount   скидка   SK@T-K@h

distance   расстояние   B@S-T@h-Y@h-NY@

doctor   врач   VB@CH

document   документ   D@h-K@-M@NT

dollar   доллар   D@-L@hB

down   вниз   VN@S

downtown   центр   TS@NTB

drink (beverage)   напиток   N@h-P@-T@K

drugstore   аптека   @P-T@@-K@h

dry cleaner   химчистка   H@M-CH@ST-K@h

duck   утка   @T-K@h

E

ear   ухо   @-H@h

ear drops   ушные капли   @SH-N@-Y@ K@h-PL@

early   рано   B@h-N@h

east   восток   V@h-ST@K

easy лёгкий L⒠ⓄH-K⒠

eat (to) есть Y⒠ST

egg яйцо Y⒠-TSⓄ

electricity электричество
⒠-L⒠K-TR⒠-CH⒠ST-V⒜

elevator лифт L⒠FT

embassy посольство P⒜-SⓄL-STV⒜

England Англия ⒜N-GL⒠-⒜

English (nationality) Англичанин
⒜N-GL⒠-CH⒜-N⒠N

enough! хватит! HV⒜-T⒠T

entrance вход FHⓄT

envelope конверт K⒜N-V⒠⒠BT

evening вечер V⒠⒠-CH⒠B

everything всё FSYⓄ

excellent отлично ⒜T-L⒠CH-N⒜

excuse me! извините! ⒠Z-V⒠-N⒠-T⒠⒠

exit выход V⒠-H⒜T

expensive дорогой D⒜-B⒜-GⓄy

eye глаз GL⒜S

eye drops глазные капли
GL⒜Z-N⒠-YⓄ K⒜-PL⒠

F

face лицо LEE-TSO

far далеко Dah-LE-KO

fare цена TSE-Nah

fast быстро BEE-STRah

father отец ah-TEETS

fax, fax machine телефакс TE-Le-FahKS

February февраль FEV-Bah'L

few мало Mah-Lah

film (movie) фильм FEELM

film (photographic) плёнка PLEON-Kah

finger палец Pah-LETS

fire extinguisher огнетушитель
  ahG-NEE-Too-SHEE-TEEL

fire (heat) огонь ah-GON

fire! (emergency) пожар! Pah-ZHahB

first первый PEEB-VEE

fish рыба BEE-Bah

flight полёт Pah-LOT

florist shop цветочный магазин
  TSVEE-TOCH-NEE Mah-Gah-ZEEN

flowers цветы TSVE-TEE

food еда YEE-Dah

foot ступня ST(oo)P-N(ee)(ah)

fork вилка V(ee)L-K(ah)

french fries жареная картошка
ZH(ah)-B(e)-N(ah)-Y(ah) K(ah)B-T(o)SH-K(ah)

fresh свежий SV(ee)(e)-ZH(ee)

Friday пятница P(ee)(a)T-N(ee)-TS(ah)

fried жареный ZH(ah)-B(e)-N(ee)

friend (m) друг DB(oo)K

friend (f) подруга P(ah)D-B(oo)-G(ah)

fruit фрукты FB(oo)K-T(i)

funny смешной SM(e)SH-N(oy)

G

gas station бензоколонка B(e)N-Z(ah)-K(ah)-L(o)N-K(ah)

gasoline бензин B(e)N-Z(ee)N

gate ворота V(ah)-B(o)-T(ah)

gift подарок P(ah)-D(ah)-B(ah)K

girl девушка D(ee)(e)-V(oo)SH-K(ah)

glass (drinking) стакан ST(ah)-K(ah)N

glasses (eye) очки (ah)CH-K(ee)

gloves перчатки P(e)B-CH(ah)T-K(ee)

go (to) идти (ee)D-T(ee)

gold золото Z(o)-L(ah)-T(ah)

golf   гольф   GOLF

golf course   площадка для гольфа
  PLah-SHCHaḣT-Kah   DLah   GOL-Fah

good   хорошо   Hah-Bah-SHO

good-bye   до свидания   Dah-SVEE-Daḣ-NYah

goose   гусь   GooS

grapes   виноград   VEE-Nah-GBaḣT

grateful (m)   благодарный   BLah-Gah-DaḣB-NEE

grateful (f)   благодарная   BLah-Gah-DaḣB-Nah-Yah

gray   серый   SEĒ-BEE

green   зелёный   ZĒ-LO-NEE

grocery store   гастроном   Gah-STBah-NOM

group   группа   GBoo-Pah

guide   гид   GEED

H

hair   волосы   VO-Lah-SEE

hairbrush   расчёска   Bah-SHCHYO-SKah

haircut   стрижка   STBEESH-Kah

ham   ветчина   VEE-CHEE-Naḣ

hamburger   гамбургер   GaḣM-BoȯB-GEB

hand   кисть   KEEST

happy (m)   счастливый   SHCHEES-LEĒ-VEE

happy (f) счастливая SHCHⒺⒺS-LⒺⒺ-Vⓐ-Yⓐ

have (I) у меня есть ⓞⓞ-MⒺⒺ-NYⓐ YⓔST

he он ⓄN

head голова Gⓐ-Lⓐ-Vⓐ

headache головная боль Gⓐ-LⓐV-Nⓐ-Yⓐ BⓄL

health club (gym) фитнес клуб
FⒺⒺT-NⓔS KLⓞⓞP

heart condition болезнь сердца
Bⓐ-LⓋⒶ-ZⓄN SⒺⓇ-TSⓐ

heart сердце SⒺⓇ-TSⒺ

heat жара ZHⓐ-Rⓐ

hello (telephone greeting) алло ⓐ-LⓄ

help! (emergency) помогите! Pⓐ-Mⓐ-GⒺⒺ-TⒺⒺ

holiday праздник PRⓐZ-NⒺⒺK

hospital больница Bⓐ-NⒺⒺ-TSⓐ

hotel гостиница Gⓐ S-TⒺⒺ-NⒺⒺ-TSⓐ

hour час CHⓐS

how как Kⓐ K

hurry up! скорее! SKⓐ-RⒺ-YⒺ

husband муж MⓞⓞSH

I

I я Yⓐ

ice лёд LⒺⓄD

ice cream мороженое Mah-BO-ZHÊ-Nah-YÊ

ice cubes кубики льда KOO-BÊÊ-KÊÊ-LDah

ill (m) болен BO-LÊN

ill (f) больна BahL-Nah

important важный Vah́ZH-NÊÊ

indigestion расстройство желудка
Bah́S-TROY-STVah ZHÊÊ-LOOT-Kah

information информация
ÊÊN-FahR-Mah́-TSÊÊ-Yah

interpreter переводчик PÊ-RÊ-VO-CHÊÊK

J

jacket пиджак PÊÊD-ZHah́K

jam джем DZHÊM

January январь Yah́N-Vah́B

jewelry драгоценности DBah-Gah-TSẾ-Nah-STÊÊ

jewelry store ювелирный магазин
YOO-VÊÊ-LÊÊB-NÊÊ Mah-Gah-ZÊÊN

job работа Bah-BO-Tah

juice сок SOK

July июль ÊÊ-YOOL

June июнь ÊÊ-YOON

K

ketchup кетчуп KÊ-CHOOP

key ключ KLY⁰⁰CH

kiss поцелуй P@h-TS@-L⁰⁰EE

knife нож N⓪SH

know (to) знать ZN@hT

L

ladies' room женский туалет
ZH©N-SK© T⁰⁰@h-L©©T

ladies' женский ZH©N-SK©

lamb баранина B@h-B@h-N©-N@h

language язык Y©-Z©K

large крупный KB⁰⁰P-N©

late поздно P⓪Z-N@h

laundry прачечная PB@h-CH©CH-N@h-Y@h

lawyer адвокат @hD-V@h-K@hT

left (direction) левый L©-V©

leg нога N@h-G@h

lemon лимон L©-M⓪N

less меньше M©©N-SH©

letter письмо P©S-M⓪

lettuce салат S@h-L@hT

like (to) мне нравится MN©© NB@h-V©T-S@h

lip губа G⁰⁰-B@h

lipstick губная помада
   GOOB-N@h-Y@h P@h-M@h-D@h

little (amount) немножко   N@M-NOSH-K@h

little (size) маленький   M@h-L@N-K@

live (to) жить   ZH@T

lobster омар   @h-M@B

long длинный   DL@-N@

love (to) любить   L@oo-B@T

luck удача   oo-D@h-CH@h

luggage багаж   B@h-G@hSH

lunch обед   @h-B@@T

M

maid горничная   GOB-N@CH-N@h-Y@h

mail почта   POCH-T@h

makeup косметика   K@hS-M@@-T@-K@h

man мужчина   Moo-SHCH@-N@h

map карта   K@B-T@h

March март   M@hBT

market рынок   B@-N@K

match (light) спичка   SP@CH-K@h

May май   M①

mayonnaise майонез   M①@-N@S

meal еда   Y@-D@h

meat мясо M(EE)(ah)-S(ah)

mechanic механик M(EE)-H(ah)-N(EE)K

meeting встреча FSTR(E)-CH(ah)

mens' restroom мужской туалет
M(oo)SH-SK(oy) T(oo)(ah)-L(EE)T

menu меню M(EE)-NY(oo)

message записка Z(ah)-P(EE)S-K(ah)

milk молоко M(ah)-L(ah)-K(O)

mineral water минеральная вода
M(EE)-N(EE)-R(ah)L-N(ah)-Y(ah) V(ah)-D(ah)

minute минута M(EE)-N(oo)-T(ah)

Miss госпожа G(ah)S-P(ah)-ZH(ah)

mistake ошибка (ah)-SH(EE)P-K(ah)

misunderstanding непонимание
N(EE)-P(ah)-N(EE)-M(ah)-NY(E)

moment момент M(ah)-M(EE)NT

Monday понедельник P(ah)-N(EE)-D(EE)L-N(EE)K

money деньги D(E)N-G(EE)

month месяц M(E)-S(EE)TS

monument памятник P(ah)-M(EE)T-N(EE)K

more больше B(O)L-SH(E)

morning утро (oo)-TR(ah)

mosque мечеть M(EE)-CH(E)T

mother мать M(ah)T

mountain   гора   G@h-R@h

movies   кино   K@-N@

Mr.   господин   G@S-P@h-D@N

Mrs.   госпожа   G@S-P@h-ZH@h

much   много   MN@-G@h

museum   музей   M@-Z@

mushrooms   грибы   GR@-B@

music   музыка   M@-Z@-K@h

mustard   горчица   G@h-R-CH@-TS@h

N

nail polish   лак для ногтей   L@K DLY@h N@K-TY@

name   имя   @-MY@h

napkin   салфетка   S@L-F@T-K@h

near   близо   BL@S-K@h

neck   шея   SH@-Y@h

need (to)   мне нужен   MN@ N@-ZH@N

never   никогда   N@-K@hG-D@h

newspaper   газета   G@h-Z@-T@h

news stand   газетный киоск   G@h-Z@T-N@ K@-@SK

night   ночь   N@CH

nightclub   ночной клуб   N@CH-N@ KL@P

no   нет   N@T

non smoking некуряший NẼE-Kọọ-R̃EẼ-SHCH̃E

noon полдень PÕL-D̃EN

north север S̃EẼ-ṼER

notary нотариус N@h-T@h-R̃EE-ọọS

November ноябрь N@h-Y@hBR̃

now сейчас S̃E-CH@hS

number номер NÕ-M̃ER

nurse медсестра M̃ET-S̃EE-STR@h

O

occupied занято Z@h-ÑEE-T@h

ocean океан @h-K̃EE-@hN

October октябрь @hK-T̃E@h-BR̃

officer офицер @h-F̃EE-TS̃ER

oil масло M@hS-L@h

omelet омлет @hM-L̃ẼET

one-way (traffic) одностороннее движение
@hD-N@h-ST@h-RÕ-Ñ̃EE DṼEE-ZH̃E-Ñ̃EE-ỸE

onion лук LọọK

open открыто @hT-KR̃ẼE-T@h

opera опера Õ-P̃E-R@h

operator телефонистка T̃E-L̃E-F@h-Ñ̃EEST-K@h

orange (color) оранжевый @h-R@hN-ZH̃E-ṼEE

order (to) заказывать Z@h-K@h-Z̃EE-V@hT

original оригинальный   ah-REE-GEE-Nah'L-NEE

owner владелец   VLah-DEE'-LOTS

oysters устрицы   oo-STREE-TSEE

P

package посылка   Pah-SEEL-Kah

paid оплачено   ah-PLah-CHE-Nah

pain боль   BOL

painting картина   Kah-TEE-Nah

paper бумага   Boo-Mah-Gah

parking стоянка   STah-Yah'N-Kah

partner (business) партнёр   PahBT-NOOB

party вечеринка   VE-CHE-BEEN-Kah

passenger пассажир   Pah-Sah-ZHEEB

passport паспорт   Pah'S-PahBT

pasta макароны   Mah-Kah-BO-NEE

pastry пирожное   PEE-BOZH-Nah-YE

pen ручка   Boo'CH-Kah

pencil карандаш   Kah-Bah'N-Dah'SH

pepper перец   PE-BOTS

perfume духи   Doo-HEE

person человек   CHE-Lah-VEEK

pharmacist аптекарь   ahP-TEE-KahB

pharmacy аптека ⓐP-Tⓔⓔ-Kⓐh

phone book телефонная книга
Tⓔⓔ-Lⓔⓔ-FⓄ-Nⓐh-Yⓐh KNⓔⓔ-Gⓐh

photo снимок SNⓔⓔ-Mⓐ̇K

photographer фотограф Fⓐh-TⓄ-GRⓐhF

pillow подушка Pⓐh-DⓞⓞSH-Kⓐh

pink розовый RⓄ-Zⓐh-Vⓔⓔ

pizza пицца Pⓔⓔ-TSⓐh

plastic (n) пластмасса PLⓐhS-Mⓐ̇-Sⓐh

plate тарелка Tⓐh-RⓔⓔⓁ-Kⓐh

please пожалуйста Pⓐh-ZHⓐ̇-Lⓞⓞ-STⓐh

pleasure удовольствие ⓞⓞ-Dⓐh-VⓄLST-Vⓔⓔ-Yⓔ

police милиция Mⓔⓔ-Lⓔⓔ-TSⓔⓔ-Yⓐh

police station отделение милиции
ⓐh-Dⓔⓔ-Lⓔ-NYⓔ Mⓔⓔ-LⓔⓔT-Sⓔⓔ-ⓔⓔ

pork свинина SVⓔⓔ-Nⓔⓔ-Nⓐh

porter носильщик Nⓐh-SⓔⓔL-SHCHⓔⓔK

post office почта PⓄCH-Tⓐh

postcard открытка ⓐhT-KRⓔⓔT-Kⓐh

potatoes картофель KⓐhR-TⓄ-Fⓔ̇L

pregnant беременная Bⓔⓔ-Rⓔ-Mⓔ-Nⓐh-Yⓐh

prescription рецепт от врача
Rⓔ-TSⓔPT ⓐhT-VRⓐh-CHⓐ̇

price цена TS®-N@h

problem проблема PR@h-BL®®-M@h

profession профессия PR@h-F®-S®-Y@h

public (n) публика P⊚B-L®-K@h

public telephone телефонавтомат
  T®-L®-FON @hF-T@h-M@hT

purified чистый CH®S-T®

purple фиолетовый F®@h-L®-T@h-V®

purse сумка S⊚M-K@h

Q

quality качество K@h-CH®ST-V@h

question вопрос V@h-PROS

quickly быстро B®-STR@h

quit (to) бросать BR@h-S@hT

quiet! (be) тихо! T®-H@h

R

radio радио R@h-D®-O

railroad железная дорога
  ZH®-L®®Z-N@h-Y@h D@h-RO-G@h

rain дождь DOSHT

raincoat плащ PL@hSHCH

ramp съезд S®®ST

razor blade лезвие L®®Z-V®-Y®

ready готово G@ĥ-TŌ-V@ĥ

receipt чек CHĒK

recommend (to) рекомендовать
RĒ-K@ĥ-MĒN-D@ĥ-V@ĥT

red красный KR@ĥŚ-NĒ

repeat! повторите! P@ĥF-T@ĥ-RĒ-TĒ

reservation бронирование
BR@ĥ-NĒ-R@ĥ-V@ĥ-NĒ-YĒ

restaurant ресторан RĒ-ST@ĥ-R@ĥN

return (to) вернуться V@B-NōōT-S@ĥ

rice (cooked) рис RĒĒS

rich богатый B@ĥ-G@ĥ-TĒ

right (correct) правильно PR@ĥ-VĒĒL-N@ĥ

right (direction) правый PR@ĥ-VĒĒ

road дорога D@ĥ-RŌ-G@ĥ

room комната KŌM-N@ĥ-T@ĥ

round trip туда и обратно
Tōō-D@ĥ ĒĒ @ĥ-BR@ĥT-N@ĥ

Russia Россия R@ĥ-SĒĒ-Y@ĥ

S

safe (hotel) сейф S@F

salad салат S@ĥ-L@ĥT

sale распродажа R@ĥS-PR@ĥ-D@ĥ́-ZH@ĥ

salmon сёмга   SYOM-Gah

salt соль   SOL

sandwich бутерброд   Boo-TEB-BROT

Saturday суббота   Soo-BO-Tah

scissors ножницы   NOZH-Nee-TSee

sculpture скульптура   SKooLP-Too-Bah

seafood морепродукты   MO-Be-PBah-Dook-Tee

season сезон   See-ZON

seat (n) место   Mees-Tah

secretary секретарь   See-KBee-Tah̆B

section отдел   ah-Deel

September сентябрь   SeN-Teah-BB

service обслуживание   ahP-SLoo-ZHee-Vah-Nee-Ye

several несколько   Nees-Kah̆L-Kah

shampoo шампунь   SHah̆M-Poon

sheets (bed) постельное бельё
Pah̆S-TeL-Nah-Ye   Bee-LYO

shirt рубаша   Boo-BahSH-Kah̆

shoes ботинки   Bah-TeeN-Kee

shoe store обувной магазин
ah-BooV-Noy̆   Mah-Gah-ZeeN

shopping center торговый центр
Tah̆B-GO-Vee   TSeNTB

shower душ   DooSH

shrimp креветки KREE-VEET-KEE

sick (m) больной BahL-Noy

sick (f) больная BahL-Nah-Yah

sign (display) знак ZNahK

signature подпись POT-PEES

silence! тишина! TEE-SHEE-Nah

single (unmarried) (m) холостой HLah-SToy

single (unmarried) (f) незамужяя
   NEE-Zah-MooZH-NEE-Yah

sir сэр SaB

sister сестра SEES-TRah

size размер RahZ-MeeR

skin кожа KO-ZHah

skirt юбка YooP-Kah

sleeve рукав Roo-KahF

slowly медленно MEED-Le-Nah

small маленький Mah-LEEN-KEE

smile (to) улыбаться oo-LEE-Bah-TSah

smoke (to) курить Koo-REET

soap мыло MWEE-Lah

socks носки NahS-KEE

some несколько NEES-Kah-Lah

something что-нибудь SHTO-NEE-BooT

sometimes иногда ⒠-NⓐG-Dⓐ

soon скоро SKⓄ-Rⓐ

sorry (pardon me) простите PRⓐS-Tⓔ-Tⓔ

soup суп S⬤P

south юг Y⬤K

souvenir сувенир S⬤-Vⓔ-NⓔR

Spanish испанский ⒠-SPⓐN-SKⒺ

specialty фирменное блюдо
   FⒺR-Mⓔ-Nⓐ-Yⓔ BLY⬤-Dⓐ

speed скорость SKⓄ-RⓐST

spoon ложка LⓄZH-Kⓐ

sport спорт SPⓄRT

spring (season) весна VⓔS-Nⓐ

stairs лестница LⓔⓔS-NⒺ-TSⓐ

stamp марка MⓐR-Kⓐ

station станция STⓐN-TSⒺ-Yⓐ

steak бифштекс BⒺF-SHTⓔKS

steamed паровой Pⓐ-Rⓐ-VⓄ

stop! стоп! STⓄP

store магазин Mⓐ-Gⓐ-ZⒺN

storm шторм SHTⓄRM

straight ahead прямо PRⒺⓐ-Mⓐ

strawberry клубника KL⬤B-NⒺ-Kⓐ

street улица   OO-LEE-TSah

string верёвка   VEH-ROV-Kah

subway метро   MEH-TRO

sugar сахар   Sah-HahR

suit (clothes) костюм   Kah S-TEE OO M

suitcase чемодан   CHEH-Mah-DahN

summer лето   LEE EH-Tah

sun солнце   SON-TSEH

suntan lotion крем для загара
   KREE EH M DLYah Zah-Gah-Rah

Sunday воскресенье   VahS-KREH-SEEN-YEH

sunglasses солнечные очки
   SOL-NEE EH CH-NEE-YEH   ah CH-KEE

supermarket гастроном   Gah S-TRah-NOM

surprise сюрприз   SOO-PREE Z

sweet сладкий   SLah T-KEE

swim (to) плавать   PLah-Vah T

swimming pool бассейн   Bah-SEE EH N

synagogue синагога   SEE-Nah-GO-Gah

T

table стол   STOL

tampon тампон   Tah M-PON

tape (sticky) скотч   SKOCH

tape recorder магнитофон M@G-N@E-T@-F@N

tax налог N@-L@K

taxi такси T@K-S@E

tea чай CH@

telephone телефон T@-L@-F@N

television телевизор T@-L@-V@E-Z@B

temperature температура T@M-P@-B@-T@-B@

tennis тенис T@-N@S

tennis court тенисная площадка
T@-N@ES-N@-Y@ PL@-SHCH@T-K@

thank you! спасибо! SP@-S@E-B@

that тот T@T

theater (movie) кинотеатр K@E-N@-T@E-@TB

there там T@M

they они @-N@E

this это @-T@

thread нитка N@ET-K@

throat горло G@B-L@

Thursday четверг CH@T-V@@BK

ticket билет B@E-L@@T

tie галстук G@L-ST@K

time время VB@-M@@

tip (gratuity) чаевые CH@E-V@E-Y@

tire шина SHEE-Nah

toast (bread) гренка GREEEN-Kah

tobacco табак Tah-BahK

today сегодня SEE-VOD-NYah

toe палец ноги Pah-LETS Nah-GEE

together вместе VMES-Tee

toilet унитаз oo-NEE-Tahs

toilet paper туалетная бумага
Too-ah-LEEET-Nah-Yah Boo-Mah-Gah

tomato помидор Pah-MEE-DOB

tomorrow завтра ZahF-TBah

toothache зубная боль ZooB-Nah-Yah BOL

toothbrush зубная щётка
ZooB-Nah-Yah SHCHOT-Kah

toothpaste зубная паста
ZooB-Nah-Yah PahS-Tah

toothpick зубочистка Zoo-Bah-CHEEST-Kah

tour поездка Pah-YEST-Kah

tourist турист Too-BEEST

tourist office туристическое бюро
Too-BEES-TEE-CHEES-Kah-Ye Beoo-BO

towel полотенце Pah-Lah-TEEEN-TSe

train поезд PO-YeST

travel agency бюро путешествий
B☺☺-B☺ P☺☺-T☺-SH☺ST-V☺

traveler's check дорожный чек
D☺-B☺ZH-N☺ CH☺K

trip поездка P☺-Y☺ST-K☺

trout форель F☺-B☺L

truth правда PB☺V-D☺

Tuesday вторник FT☺B-N☺K

turkey индейка ☺N-D☺-K☺

U

umbrella зонт Z☺NT

understand (to) понимать P☺-N☺-M☺T

underwear нижнее бельё N☺ZH-N☺-Y☺ B☺-L☺

United Kingdom Великобритания
V☺-L☺-K☺-BB☺-T☺-N☺-Y☺

United States Соединённые Штаты
S☺-Y☺-D☺-NY☺-N☺-Y☺ SHT☺-T☺

university университет ☺-N☺-V☺B-S☺-T☺T

up вверх V☺BH

urgent срочный SB☺CH-N☺

V

vacant вакантный V☺-K☺NT-N☺

vacation отпуск ☺T-P☺SK

valuable ценный TS®-N®

value ценность TS®-N@ST

vanilla (flavor) ванильное V@-N®L-N@-Y®

veal телятина T®-LY@-T®-N@

vegetables овощи ©́-V@-SH®

view вид V®T

vinegar уксус ©K-S©S

voyage путешествие P©-T®-SH®́ST-V®-Y®

W

wait! подожди! P@-D@ZH-D®

waiter официант @-F®-TS@NT

waitress официантка @-F®-TS@NT-K@

want (I) я хочу Y@ H@-CH©

wash (to) мыть MW®T

watch out! осторожно! @S-T@-R©ZH-N@

water вода V@-D@́

watermelon арбуз @B-B©S

we мы MW®

weather погода P@-G©́-D@

Wednesday среда SR®-D@́

week неделя N®-D®́-LY@

weekend выходные V®-H@D-N®-Y®

welcome добро пожаловать Dah-BRO
P@h-ZH@h-L@h-VahT

well done (cooked) хорошо прожареный
H@h-R@h-SHO PR@h-ZH@h-R@-N@

west запад Z@h-P@hT

wheelchair инвалидное кресло
@N-V@h-L@D-N@h-Y@ KR@@S-L@h

when? когда? K@hG-D@h

where? где? GDY@

which? какой? K@h-K@y

white белый B@@-L@

who? кто? KT@

why? почему? P@h-CH@-M@@

wife жена ZH@-N@h

wind ветер V@@-T@R

window окно @hK-NO

wine вино V@-NO

winter зима Z@-M@h

with с SS

woman женщина ZH@N-SH@-N@h

wonderful замечательный Z@h-M@-CH@h-T@L-N@

world мир M@R

wrong неправильный N@-PR@h-V@L-N@

XYZ

year год G⦿T

yellow жёлтый ZH⦿L-T⒠

yes да D⒜

yesterday вчера FCH⒠-R⒜

you ты T⒠

zipper замок Z⒜-M⦿K

zoo зоопарк Z⒜-⒜-P⒜RK

THANKS!

The nicest thing you can say to anyone in any language is "Thank you." Try some of these languages using the incredible Vowel Symbol System.

Spanish	French
GRah-SEE-ahS	MeR-SEE

German	Italian
DahN-Kuh	GRahT-SEE-e

Japanese	Chinese
DO-MO	SHEEe SHEEe

Swedish

TⓐⓗK

Portuguese

Ⓞ-BRⒺⒺ-Gⓐⓗ-DⓄ

Arabic

SHⓞⓞ-KⓇⓐⓗN

Greek

ⓔF-Hⓐⓗ-RⒺⒺ-STⓄ

Hebrew

TⓄ-Dⓐⓗ

Russian

SPⓐⓗ-SⒺⒺ-Bⓐⓗ

Swahili

ⓐⓗ-SⓐⓗN-TⒶ

Dutch

DⓐⓗNK ⓞⓞ

Tagalog

Sⓐⓗ-Lⓐⓗ-MⓐⓗT

Hawaiian

Mⓐⓗ-Hⓐⓗ-LⓄ

INDEX

NOTES

QUICK REFERENCE PAGE

Hello

Здравствуйте (polite)

ZDRah-STVoo-Yé-Tée

How are you?

Как вы поживаете?

Kah K Vee Pah-ZHee-Vah-Yé-Tée

Yes	**No**
Да	Нет
Dah	Neet

Please

Пожалуйста

Pah-ZHah-Loo-STah

Thank you.

Спасибо.

SPah-See-Bah

I'm sorry.	**Help!**
Проститею.	Помогите!
PRah-STee-Tée	Pah-Mah-Gee-Tée

I don't understand!

Я не понимаю!

Yah Nee-Pah-Nee-Mah-Yoo
